The Unity of
Understanding

The Unity of Understanding

A Study in Kantian Problems

Hubert Schwyzer

CLARENDON PRESS · OXFORD

1990

Oxford University Press, Walton Street, Oxford OX2 6DP
Oxford New York Toronto
Delhi Bombay Calcutta Madras Karachi
Petaling Jaya Singapore Hong Kong Tokyo
Nairobi Dar es Salaam Cape Town
Melbourne Auckland
and associated companies in
Berlin Ibadan

Oxford is a trade mark of Oxford University Press

Published in the United States
by Oxford University Press, New York

British Library Cataloguing in Publication Data
Schwyzer, Hubert
The unity of understanding: a study in Kantian problems
1. Knowledge. Theories of Kant, Immanuel, 1724–1804
I. Title
121'.092'.4
ISBN 0–19–824829–6
Library of Congress Cataloguing in Publication Data
Schwyzer, Hubert
The unity of understanding: a study of Kantian problems
1. Kant, Immanuel. 1724–1804—Contributions in comprehension
(theory of knowledge)
2. Comprehension (Theory of knowledge)—History
I. Title
B2799.C78538   1989   121'.4–dc20   89–37636
ISBN 0–19–824829–6

Set by Pentacor Ltd., High Wycombe, Bucks
Printed in Great Britain by
Courier International Ltd., Tiptree, Essex

for Carol

ACKNOWLEDGEMENTS

This book had its origins in some lectures I gave at Santa Barbara on the Schematism. It was completed while I was a visitor at the University of York in 1987–8.

Various parts of the book have at various times been delivered as lectures at universities in California and in England. Chapters 2 and 3 are an extended and somewhat altered version of an article that appeared in *Kant-Studien* for 1983, under the title 'How are Concepts of Objects Possible?', and a portion of Chapter 5, called 'Sentience and Apperception', was read before the Sixth International Kant Congress at Pennsylvania State University in 1985, and subsequently published in the Proceedings of that Congress. I am indebted to the Kant-Gesellschaft for permission to reprint these items.

I owe a great deal to the friends, colleagues, and students whose thoughts have stimulated and influenced mine over the years; in particular to Noel Fleming, without whose encouragement I might never have taught a course on Kant, to Richard Bosley, Francis Dauer, Bill Forgie, Lloyd Reinhardt, Merrill Ring, Stephen Simon, and most especially to my wife Carol. I should also like to thank Meredith Sedgwick, who typed the various drafts of this book, for a wonderful combination of patience, cheerfulness, and efficiency.

H.S.

Santa Barbara, California
September 1988

CONTENTS

1. Introduction   1
2. How are Concepts of Objects Possible?   6
3. A Reconsideration   32
4. The Idea of a Transcendental Deduction   49
5. Sentience, Apperception, and Language   61
6. Consciousness as Rule-Governed   113
7. Conclusion   162
   Index   169

1

Introduction

This book is about Kant's account of the nature of human understanding. But it is not a general treatment of any part of Kant's philosophy, nor a commentary of any kind. It is an attempt, rather, to get clear about the philosophical aims and convictions that are embedded in Kant's account, and about the problems that it is designed to solve. I think Kant's is a deeply attractive theory. I believe that the problems it sets for itself are genuine and important philosophical problems, and that its proposed solutions to them are essentially on the right lines. Nevertheless, I am convinced that Kant's theory, as it stands, does not and cannot succeed in solving these problems. So I am interested in what it is about it that prevents it from succeeding, and in whether anything can be done about this without departing from those aims and convictions which guide what Kant has to say.

For Kant, the understanding is the capacity to become conscious of objects, to bring things before the mind. This capacity is exercised both when we are actually aware of a particular object, for example when we see it before our eyes, and also when, in its absence, we think about it. There is nothing in this, so far, that sharply separates Kant from his philosophical predecessors; they too would assign these tasks to the understanding. It is on the question of *how understanding arises*, of how we are to explain our awareness of things and our ability to think of them, that Kant, quite rightly, believed his position to be essentially different from and radically opposed to those of the earlier philosophers. For on all those earlier views, whether rationalist or empiricist, realist or idealist, our consciousness of things and our ideas of them depend in one way or another upon, and are explained with reference to, the things themselves. This is so, whether the way in which those things are presented to us is conceived to be sensory (as with Locke or Hume), or intellectual (Descartes or Leibniz); and whether the objects at issue are thought to exist independently of the mind they confront (Descartes, Locke), or not (Hume). It is on this general issue of the dependence of understanding on its objects that Kant parts company with the earlier philosophers.

So we have, as a beginning point, the following largely negative thesis to guide Kant's account of the nature of understanding.

. 1. Human understanding is essentially something autonomous, not something that is a response to, or that conforms to, something else. Neither our consciousness of things nor our capacity to form concepts of them can be explained by reference to any confrontation, intellectual or sensible, that we might have with them. In particular, there is no consciousness of anything that consists simply in our being sensorily affected, and there is no concept so basic, no idea so 'simple', that it arises merely from our receiving sense-impressions. Understanding is never a kind of recording, or following, or mirroring, or matching; it is from first to last 'spontaneous'.

Kant is aware that this 'spontaneity'-thesis raises a problem which his predecessors did not have to meet, namely that of accounting for how understanding can be *of* objects at all, and in particular of empirical objects. So we have a second thesis.

2. Despite its spontaneity, our understanding is not cut loose from its objects. It is, by its own nature (that is, a priori) capable of attaching to just those things we see and touch which themselves cannot, according to 1, be regarded as responsible for it.

And to this pair of theses Kant adds a third, of equal importance.

3. Our understanding is necessarily expressible in the language with which we communicate with one another.

There is no essentially subjective understanding, there is no grasping in consciousness which does not obey the rules or conditions governing the general intelligibility of what we say. It is not something extraneous and additional to the fact of our understanding that we are able to express that understanding by following those rules.

These theses guide Kant's account of understanding in the sense that his account is an attempt to work out the nature of understanding—to answer the question of how consciousness and thought of objects is possible—given those three theses. But those theses do not of course constitute a set of unproved assumptions for Kant. He means to argue for each of them. And if his argument for them is to be successful, it is not enough that he should have, as he does have, plausible and important things to say about each of the three aspects of understanding at issue, namely spontaneity, the relation to objects, and intelligibility. It is also necessary that he should be able to explain how these different features are connected with one another so as to be aspects of a single thing. For it is, crucially, one and the same thing, consciousness of objects, that our triad of theses declares to be spontaneous, related a priori to objects, and subject to the rules of intelligibility. But Kant, I shall maintain, is unable to explain these connections. We will see that he is repeatedly obliged to make *ad hoc* manœuvres and adjustments in order to try to meet the different demands made by the three theses, and that he cannot, in the end, show how it is that one and the same capacity, univocally called 'understanding', can be responsible for the variety of different tasks required of it.[1] Kant in fact gives

---

[1] Though Kant is clearly aware of the need for unity here. See e.g. A126: 'We have already defined understanding in various ways: as spontaneity of knowledge . . . as a power of thought, as a faculty of concepts, or again of judgments. *All these definitions, when they are adequately understood, are identical*' (italics added). He immediately goes on to call it also the 'faculty of rules' and, later, the 'faculty of apperception' (B134 n.), and he certainly intends his identity claim to cover these formulations as well. What this need for identity, or unity, specifically amounts to, and what its various ramifications are, is something that will become clear as we proceed. It is by no means a merely academic issue, at home only in the jargon of 'faculty psychology'.

us three distinct theories rather than one: a theory of what it is to be aware of anything (the Transcendental Deduction), a theory of how concepts are applied (the Schematism), and a theory of how propositions are formed (the Clue to the Discovery of All Pure Concepts of the Understanding). And all we have to connect these theories with one another is Kant's unargued insistence that they are all partial theories of one and the same thing.

I shall try to show that Kant's inability to explain these crucial connections is deeply rooted in his philosophical orientation to the mind. The requirements he lays down for understanding (our three theses) cannot be satisfied within that general picture of what it is to be a conscious being which he inherits from his predecessors, and which he has not fully succeeded in eliminating from his own position. This is the picture, deriving from Descartes, according to which the fundamental fact of consciousness, a fact in no way to be further explained or analysed, is the phenomenon of *representing something to oneself*. A conscious being, on this view, is, at bottom, a being capable of such representing (where 'at bottom' means that this capability cannot itself be further spelled out).

That Cartesian conception of consciousness which continues to lurk uncritically at the back of Kant's theory is, we shall see, irretrievably subjective, and so quite unregimentable. There is no possible argument to the effect that representing-something-to-oneself, where that is taken to be an *Urphänomen*, must satisfy the conditions laid down by Kant, or for that matter, any conditions whatever. In particular, there is no possibility of making out that being conscious of something, so understood, contains an a priori relation to objects on the one hand (thesis 2), and is subject to rules on the other (thesis 3). I hope to be able to show that Kant's three

The references above are to *Critique of Pure Reason*, trans. Norman Kemp Smith, (London, 1929). I follow the standard practice of giving references by the pagination of the first (A) and second (B) editions (Riga, 1781, 1787). In quoting from the *Critique* I will occasionally depart from Kemp Smith, particularly on the rendering of *'erkennen'* and *'Erkenntnis'* (see ch. 4 below).

theses provide a powerful tool, not only for criticizing that Cartesian picture of consciousness, but also for mapping out a viable alternative to it. What is called for, by our three theses, is a different picture, of a quite specific kind. This is one which portrays our capacity to represent things to ourselves, not as something fundamental, and fundamentally subjective, about which nothing further can be said, but as constituted by a certain fully objective fact of our nature. I introduce this picture in a preliminary and hypothetical way in Chapter 3, and argue for it more fully in Chapter 6.

My text is, for the most part, the *Critique of Pure Reason*, and in particular the first three chapters of the Transcendental Analytic, namely those containing the Clue, the Transcendental Deduction, and the Schematism. It is an important part of my project to spell out as clearly as I can the problems which Kant is wrestling with in these chapters, and to try to show both why they are important problems, and that Kant's approach to them is generally correct. If I cannot do this I cannot show the strength and plausibility of the three theses about the understanding that are at issue. Yet there are standard questions and reservations about what Kant seems to be trying to do in each of these chapters. The argument of the Clue, the so-called 'metaphysical deduction' of the categories from the judgment forms, is obscure and is often thought to be quite wrongheaded. The point of the Transcendental Deduction is far from clear, as is also its relation to the Clue on the one hand and the Schematism on the other. And it needs to be shown why a doctrine of Schematism is necessary at all.

I begin, for reasons of expository convenience and clarity, with the idea of Schematism.

2

How are Concepts of Objects Possible?

At the beginning of the Analytic of Principles in the *Critique of Pure Reason* Kant distinguishes the faculty of judgment from the faculty of understanding (see A132/B171). This comes as a surprise: hitherto, in the preceding Analytic of Concepts, we had been led to believe that the understanding was sufficient for a whole range of intellectual activity, and in particular that acts of judgment were well within that range. But now we are told that whereas understanding is the faculty of concepts (or rules), judgment is the faculty of *subsuming under* concepts (or rules). Having made this distinction, Kant sets himself the task of determining how, given the character of our concepts, as described so far, subsumption under them is possible. The chapter on Schematism is designed to answer this question.

Kant's distinction between understanding and judgment is, when not ignored in the literature[1] frequently criticized, and, it might seem, for good reason. For it sounds as if Kant is telling us that it is in general one thing to have a concept, or to understand a rule, and quite another thing to be able to apply that concept, or rule, to anything. Jonathan Bennett, for one, finds this 'unacceptable'.

---

[1] Ignored, e.g. by P. F. Strawson, *The Bounds of Sense* (London, 1966). Criticized explicitly and directly by Jonathan Bennett in *Kant's Analytic* (Cambridge, 1966); see below. Somewhat less directly by G. J. Warnock, 'Concepts and Schematism', *Analysis*, 1949, and T. E. Wilkerson, *Kant's Critique of Pure Reason* (Oxford, 1976). And implicitly by H. A. Prichard, *Kant's Theory of Knowledge* (Oxford, 1909).

I might possess a concept but be unable to apply it because it had no instances or because a sensory disability prevented me from recognizing its instances. But I could not possess a concept yet be unable to apply it because of an intellectual defect, a defect in my 'judgment', ... Having a concept involves being able both to use it in 'rules' and, under favourable sensory circumstances, to apply it to its instances. You will not credit me with having the concept of a dog just because I can state many general truths about dogs, such as that they are mammals, never laugh, have legs, etc. If I can do this and yet—although not sensorily disabled—apply the word 'dog' to particular birds, humans, porpoises, etc., and often apply 'not a dog' to particular dogs, you must conclude that I do not understand 'mammals', 'laugh', 'legs', etc. But in that case my stock of 'general truths about dogs' is like a parrot's repertoire: it is not evidence that I understand the word 'dog' in any way at all.[2]

Kant, says Bennett, has the mistaken 'idea that the understanding is limited to the use of concepts in "rules",' or general propositions, that the ability to use a concept in rules is 'sufficient as well as necessary for concept possession'.[3] If Bennett is right here, then the question which the doctrine of Schematism is designed to answer fails to be a genuine one. There can be no question of how, given that I have mastered the use of a concept in rules, I go about the business of applying the concept to its instances. For unless one already knew how to, had the intellectual ability to, apply the concept, then whatever one did could not amount to using the concept in rules.

What Bennett claims about what is involved in the possession of a concept seems to me to be essentially correct; one's capacity to apply concepts is not a discrete capacity over and above one's having concepts: to have a concept is, in general and *ceteris paribus*,[4] to be able to apply it. If one could not apply it one could not be said to understand anything by its means.

But I do not think Bennett is at all right in supposing

---

[2] Bennett, *Kant's Analytic*, p. 146.
[3] Ibid.
[4] Lauchlan Chipman has argued that one might have certain concepts and

that Kant failed to see this. It is true that Kant often talks
as if one might have concepts without, yet, having the
ability to apply them. That is, he often, even usually,
calls the unschematized categories (these are the items
which lack criteria of application) 'concepts', and he
sometimes (though atypically) talks as if understanding
were somehow independent of judgment. But, on the
other hand, there are numerous passages, in the *Critique*
and elsewhere, where he emphatically insists that unschematized categories are not concepts of anything at
all, that nothing is understood by their means. Without
their schemata, he says, the categories 'would be void of
all content, and therefore mere logical forms, not pure
concepts of the understanding' (A136/B175); they 'can
find no object, and so can acquire no meaning which
might yield a concept of some object . . . [they] are merely
functions of the understanding for concepts' (A147/
B186–7). Again: the unschematized category 'can contain
nothing but the logical function for bringing the manifold under a concept' (A245). '. . .they are themselves
nothing but logical functions, and as such do not produce
the least concept of an object . . .'.[5]

These remarks, and others like them,[6] strongly suggest
that Kant's reason for holding that the categories need to
be schematized is not that he believes that something
over and above the having of a concept is required for one
to be able to apply that concept, but rather that he
believes that the unschematized categories are not as
such (or yet) concepts of anything. Whatever it is that one
possesses in possessing an unschematized category, on
Kant's view, it is not, *pace* Bennett, sufficient for concept
possession. (And there is certainly no indication that
Kant believed that one can have an *empirical* concept,

yet be unable to apply them—concepts of relatively unfamiliar things, like
that of a tadpole or of bone-marrow. See his 'Kant's Categories and Their
Schematism', *Kant-Studien*, 1972.

[5] *Prolegomena to Any Future Metaphysics*, ed. by Lewis White Beck
(Indianapolis, 1950), 71.
[6] See particularly the first half of the chapter on Phenomena and Noumena
(A239/B298–A248/B305); and also e.g. A349, A399 ff., A567/B595.

like that of a dog—as in Bennett's example—without being able to apply it.)

We should not be misled by the fact that Kant so frequently, when he is less directly concerned with their status, calls the unschematized categories 'concepts'. His doing so can be explained by the fact that he is often looking ahead—the categories will after all eventually, when schematized, be genuine concepts—and not paying specific attention to the fact that they are as yet unschematized. (Kant is, moreover, far from scrupulous about what things he is unselfconsciously prepared to call 'concepts'. A striking case of this is at B40, where he blithely talks of the concept of space immediately after he has declared it to be an intuition, not a concept.)

My first goal is to argue that Kant's distinction between understanding and judgment is not the spurious separation of the application of concepts from their possession. It is, instead, a valid and important distinction between elements contained *within* the intellectual capacity we call the possession of concepts, between sub-faculties of the faculty of understanding, broadly so called.[7]
The Analytic of Concepts deals with the former of these elements (the category, the 'logical function for bringing the manifold under a concept'); the Analytic of Principles, particularly the chapter on Schematism, deals with the latter (the schema). The initial identification and characterization of the categories, in the Analytic of Concepts, is not, as Bennett supposes it to be,[8] a description of certain fully fledged fundamental concepts (of Substance, Cause, etc.); but rather a *partial* description of what is fundamentally involved in having concepts, not only of substance, cause, etc., but of anything at all.

I believe that Kant in fact agrees with Bennett as to the dual character of concept possession. Bennett claims

[7] Kant conceived of understanding sometimes in a broader, sometimes in a narrower sense, depending on the contrast (with sensibility, with judgment) he wished to draw. Cp. A132/B171 with e.g. A69/B94.

[8] *Kant's Analytic*, pp. 76 ff., 148 ff.

(p. 146) that 'Having a concept involves being able both to use it in "rules" and, under favourable sensory circumstances, to apply it to its instances.' We can imagine Kant claiming: 'Having a concept involves being able both to use it according to the rules specified in the Analytic of Concepts, and also to apply it to spatio-temporal objects in accordance with the application conditions given in the Analytic of Principles.' If this is correct, then the point of disagreement between Bennett and Kant is not, as Bennett supposes it to be, on the issue of whether the two capacities in question are internal to the having of a concept. They agree on this. Yet Kant believes that there is nevertheless a question—the question for the chapter of Schematism—as to how application of concepts is possible. Bennett maintains that there can be no legitimate question of this kind. Indeed, he seems to hold that Kant's 'problem' here stems precisely from a *failure* to recognize that both abilities are involved in concept possession. Who is right here? Does the chapter on Schematism address a real problem, or does it not? And what accounts for this disagreement?

To answer these questions we must first look more closely at what the dual nature of concept possession is supposed to consist in. The second member of the pair of elements seems, on the surface at least, straightforward enough: one must be able to apply, subsume things under, the concept in question; one must, in a practical, recognitional sense,[9] know the conditions that must hold for the concept to apply to things. It is the first member of the pair that seems to need clarifying. The question is: just what is a concept considered apart from the conditions of its application to things? What is an unschematized, a yet-to-be-schematized, category?[10]

---

[9] It is not enough to be able only to *say* what the conditions are. That would be a matter of knowing rules and so, it seems, would belong on the other side of the duality.

[10] How, it might be asked, can we so simply equate 'concept (in general)' with 'category' here? The answer is that for Kant any concept divested of its application conditions *is* a category. The concept 'dog', considered altogether apart from the conditions of its application to things in the world, is nothing but the unschematized category 'substance'. We shall have more to say about this in Ch. 3.

Bennett's 'use of a concept in "rules" ' does not, even in principle, capture what Kant has in mind. What Bennett means by this phrase, or, at least, most of what he means by it, is clear from the long quotation from his book that we gave earlier. The ability to use a concept (that of a dog) in 'rules' is there explained as the ability to state (many) general truths about dogs. Other passages (e.g. pp. 87 f.) show that he also wishes to include (true) past-tense statements in this use of a concept.[11] The ability to make statements of these two kinds is contrasted with—and here we have the other side of the duality—the ability to apply words to 'presented bits of the world' (p. 84). And this latter ability is characterized as the ability to make statements of the form 'This is . . .', and 'That is . . .'— statements which are mere 'responses to, or operations upon, the environment in which they are made' (p. 87). So Bennett reads Kant as distinguishing between abilities to make different kinds of statements. To have the yet-to-be schematized category is to be able to make general ('rule-like') and past-tense statements which are, as it were, at some remove from presented reality; to be able to apply concepts is to be able to make statements which are direct responses to or recordings of what is presented.

I think it is clear that *if* Bennett were right in this characterization of Kant's distinction, then the separation of understanding and judgment would indeed be, as he claims, unjustified, and the problem for Schematism, the problem of how subsumption is possible, would be a spurious one. 'Kant is entitled to distinguish between rule-like judgments and others, but not to say that the understanding is concerned solely with the former' (p. 146), for if one's understanding consisted solely in the

---

[11] Bennett claims (*Kant's Analytic*, p. 87) that it is general statements and statements about the past that mark human languages as 'concept-exercising' ones. And he says (p. 88), 'Throughout the *Critique* when Kant speaks of "judgments", of "concepts" and of "understanding", he is unquestionably referring to the area of intellectual competence which is roughly marked off by the phrase "concept-exercising language".' Bennett gives no evidence for his belief that Kant connected this area of intellectual competence specifically with the ability to cope with generality and the past. One rather suspects that he is here attributing to Kant his own interesting theory, from *Rationality* (London, 1964).

capacity to make rule-like statements, if one could not also apply one's language to presented bits of the world, then one's stock of such statements would be 'like a parrot's repertoire'. The ability to make rule-like statements already includes the ability to make statements which are simply 'responses to the environment'; it cannot therefore be treated, as on Bennett's view Kant treats it, in separation from this.

Bennett's distinction may very well be an interesting and important distinction to draw, but it is not Kant's.[12] To have a yet-to-be-schematized category is not to be able to make general statements, as opposed to particular ones. It is, I shall try to show, to be able to make *coherent* or *intelligible* statements, whether general or particular, whether of the form 'All . . .', or 'Some . . .', or 'This . . .'. Conversely, to 'have' a given schema is not to be able to make particular statements ('This is . . .', 'That is . . .') corresponding to the general ones given in the matching category; it is to be able to bring to bear on the world presented to the senses a statement of whatever form, for example general *or* particular, is given in the category. Bennett, I am saying, draws the line in the wrong place. For Kant, both generality and particularity are on the side of the unschematized category. The distinction at issue is not between the ability to make one kind of statement and the ability to make another kind of statement; it is a distinction between different *aspects*, different *dimensions*, of the ability to make intelligible statements of any kind or form.

To see this, we must go back, in the *Critique*, to where the categories are first introduced, to the Clue of the Discovery of All Pure Concepts of the Understanding, the passage commonly referred to as the Metaphysical Deduction. Kant's list of categories, not yet schematized,

[12] Bennett may be right in claiming that to have a concept one must not only be able to make general (synthetic) statements, one must also know some of them to be true. And ultimately Kant will agree: to have the *schematized* categories is to be committed to the truth of certain synthetic propositions, the Principles of Pure Understanding. But this is a different issue, and sheds no light on what intellectual capacity it is that the possession of *un*schematized category consists in.

is there derived from a Table of Judgments,[13] a list of twelve propositional or judgmental forms or functions. Every proposition can be classified in four different ways, according to its 'quantity', its 'quality', its 'relation', and its 'modality'. And every proposition, it seems (Kant isn't altogether clear on this), will be of one or another of three possible forms under each of these four heads. In drawing up his list, Kant relies, he claims, on the 'labours of the logicians'.[14]

Table of Judgements

I

Quantity of Judgments

Universal
Particular
Singular

II

Quality

Affirmative
Negative
Infinite

III

Relation

Categorical
Hypothetical
Disjunctive

IV

Modality

Problematic
Assertoric
Apodeictic

Source: A70/B95

[13] This is 'judgment' in Kant's more usual sense, the sense of 'proposition', not in the special sense, of 'subsumption', in which judgment is contrasted with understanding. The two senses are connected in the following way. To judge is, in general, to compose, to put together, a thought in the mind. Sometimes Kant thinks of judgment as merely this (or as the result of merely this)—without regard to the fact that a thought is *to the effect that something (real or possible) is such and such*. At other times—as in the contrast with understanding—that fact comes to the fore. What this amounts to will become clearer as we proceed.   [14] *Prolegomena, §39.*

Before we see how the categories are meant to be derived from these judgment forms, we should spend a moment considering what Kant believes these forms to be. I do not think it is enough to regard them, as Bennett does, as 'indispensable kinds of judgment', ' "formal" features of judgments' (p. 77). At A69/B94 Kant calls the Table of Judgments an 'exhaustive statement of the functions of unity in judgments', and he introduces the forms, collectively, as 'the function of thought in judgment' (which 'can be brought under four heads each of which contains three moments') (A70/B95). Later he characterizes them (any one of them indifferently) as the 'function which gives unity to the various representations in a judgment' (A79/B104); and as 'logical functions in all possible judgments' (A79/B105). And he says that 'they specify the understanding completely, and yield an exhaustive inventory of its powers' (ibid.). He also calls them 'moments of thought in general' (A71/B96), and 'moments of thought in judgments' which 'express [*ausüben*] the functions of the understanding' (A73/B98).

These characterizations suggest to me that the Table of Judgments does more than answer the question: What, formally speaking, are the most basic kinds of judgments? Or: What are the indispensable formal features of judgments? They suggest that it serves also as an answer to questions like: What functions, or operations, of the understanding are there, as exemplified in judgments, in the formal structure of sentences? Or: By what powers or operations of the understanding (as expressed by the formal structure of sentences)—by what moments (movements) of thought—are thought-elements, representations, put together or united into a thought? The guiding idea here seems to be that since (declarative) sentences must be structured in such-and-such ways if they are to be sentences at all—if they are to express thoughts at all—one can infer operations of the understanding solely from the structure of such sentences, without any reference to their content. If one can exhaustively specify, conjunctively and disjunctively,

the features that a string of words must have in order for
it to be the expression of a thought—without taking into
account what the words stand for, or even that they stand
for anything—then one will thereby have identified the
functions or operations of the understanding, whereby
what would otherwise be a merely random sequence of
thought-elements achieves the unity, or coherence, or a
thought.

The Table of Judgments is a discovery of general
(formal) logic. It tells us what is required for thinking 'in
general'; that is, for thinking, irrespective of whatever
the subject matter might be, irrespective, indeed, of there
being any such thing as a subject-matter for thinking.
'General logic . . . abstracts from all content of knowledge, that is from all relation of knowledge to the object'
(A55/B79). Neither the nature nor the existence of a
'content' for thought is taken into account at this level.
We are concerned here solely with what we might call
the *horizontal* dimension of thought; the 'functions of
unity', the unifying, coherent-making operations of the
understanding, the rules for linking representations, or
words, with one another so as to procure that unity or
coherence. What is omitted from consideration is the
entire *vertical* dimension of thought: the linkage of
representations, or words, not with one another, but with
things in the world. The very idea of thought as having a
content or subject-matter, as being of or about anything
at all, is at this stage left deliberately out of consideration. We shall see later why it is that Kant finds it
necessary to begin his account of understanding at this
purely horizontal, contentless level.

Now, I think the step from the judgment forms to the
categories is neither as large nor as obscure as it
sometimes is made to seem. If our exposition so far has
been in outline correct we can anticipate that it is in any
case *not* the step from 'formal features of judgment' to
'fundamental concepts of objects'—a step which would
indeed be both large and obscure. For, on the one hand,
the judgment forms are considerably more than simply
formal features of judgments, and on the other hand, if

we are to give any credence at all to the remarks of Kant's that I quoted earlier, the categories are considerably less than concepts of anything.

The transition from the judgment forms to the categories introduces the *idea* of objects of thought, of a content or subject-matter for thinking, but it does, as we shall

Table of Categories

I

Of Quantity

Unity
Plurality
Totality

II

Of Quality

Reality
Negation
Limitation

III

Of Relation

Of Inherence and
Subsistence
  (*substantia et accidens*)
Of Causality and
Dependence
  (cause and effect)
Of Community
  (reciprocity between
  agent and patient)

IV

Of Modality

Possibility—Impossibility
Existence—Non-existence
Necessity—Contingency

Source: A80/B106

see, no more than this. In particular, it does *not* introduce general conditions for applying the forms to objects of experience[15], nor does it introduce concepts of objects; these, in both cases, must wait for Schematism. Whereas the judgment forms are 'logical functions in all possible judgments' (A79/B105), the categories are 'logical functions for bringing the manifold under a concept' (A245). A given category *is* the corresponding logical function, conceived now as ranging over whatever might be presented as objects of thought: 'The same function which gives unity to the various representations *in a judgment* also gives unity to the mere synthesis of various representations *in an intuition*' (A79/B105). The Table of Judgments is concerned with the question: What is it to think at all, what operations of the understanding are required for thinking 'in general'? The Table of Categories on the other hand is concerned with the question: How are we thinking *of anything that can be thought about when* we think at all, that is when we perform these same operations of the understanding? (Note: It is important not to confuse the (intentional) *objects* of thinking, what we think *of* or *about*, with the *materials* of thinking, the ideas, thought-elements, representations, things we think *with*, things which themselves are combined into thoughts by functions of the understanding.)

We can see now how it is that the categories apply a priori (i.e. necessarily) to objects of thought.[16] If the Table of Judgments has exhaustively specified the operations of the understanding, and if understanding can be about things, if it has objects at all, then those operations, conceived as having application to those objects, must in fact apply to them. If there are no other ways of thinking at all then there are no other ways of thinking about objects.

[15] See Strawson, *Bounds of Sense*, p. 76.
[16] Kant notes this as he introduces the categories: '. . .we are entitled . . . to regard them as applying a priori to objects' (A79/B105). This does not mean that the argument of the Transcendental Deduction is redundant, for it has yet to be shown that whatever we can become conscious of in experience is necessarily an object of thought. See Ch. 4.

What we should also see, and apparently this is not so easy to see, is that the not-yet-schematized-category adds to the corresponding judgment form *only the idea* of its application to objects. It tells us nothing whatever about the conditions of that application, about what such an application would amount to. The only 'content' which the categories have which the judgment forms do not have is 'whatever objects might be presented'; they, the categories, tell us nothing about what such objects are or might be like: ' . . . what sort of thing it is that demands one of these functions rather than another remains altogether undetermined' (A246). The terms 'substance', 'cause', 'totality', etc., are completely uninformative as to the nature of the objects to which they will eventually, when schematized, apply. For the only sense possessed at this stage by the category terms is the sense of the judgment forms. As Kant tells us, 'Substance . . . when the sensible determination of permanence [i.e. the schema] is omitted, would mean simply a something which can be thought only as subject, never as predicate of something else' (A147/B186).[17] And 'If I omit from the concept of cause the time in which something follows upon something else in conformity with a rule [again the schema], I should find in the pure category nothing further than that there is something from which we can conclude to the existence of something else' (A243/B301). 'I can neither put such a concept to any use, nor draw the least inference from it. For no object is thereby determined for its employment, and consequently we do not know whether it signifies anything whatever' (ibid.).

In knowing that the categories apply necessarily to objects, and in knowing what the individual categories are, we still know nothing about those objects, nothing even of a very general kind.[18] For the category terms

[17] The 'only' and 'never' here seem to be illicit. The judgment form would seem to permit only 'Thought *as* subject, *not* as predicate'. Kant is looking ahead, paving the way for the First Analogy. But that does not affect our present point: he is aware that the unschematized category does not tell us what 'sort of the thing' the object is.

[18] Cp. Bennett, *Kant's Analytic*, p. 151.

'substance', 'cause', 'totality', etc., have, as yet, no meaning with respect to objects, no 'objective' meaning, only a 'formal', or 'logical', or 'linguistic' one. A substance, a cause, a totality, etc., cannot at this stage be thought of as things of a certain kind or character; each of them is nothing more than the quite 'undetermined', unqualified, denotatum of a term which has a certain horizontal function in our thinking. What the Table of Categories brings with it which was not present in the Table of Judgments is simply the idea of there *being* a vertical as well as a horizontal dimension to thinking. But the categories do not, yet, contain any vertical pointers. Although, unlike the judgment forms, they do not 'abstract from all relation of knowledge to the object', they still tell us nothing about those objective *relata*, they contain no description of any object. (I shall have more to say soon about what 'description' means here— what Kant means by the 'determining' of an object). We are, with the categories, still confined to horizontal elements, to the function of unity, the coherent-making operations of the understanding—conceived now as having application to things. The categories, we might say, specify the horizontal features that a thought must have *if* it is to be of or about anything, if it is to have a vertical dimension.

If the foregoing is a correct account of the nature of the categories as originally introduced in the *Critique*, as derived from the judgment forms, then Kant is right, I submit, in supposing that there is a further step that he must take to complete his story of the workings of the understanding with regard to things in the world. If we are to conceive anything by means of the categories, if they are to be concepts of anything (actual or possible) at all, then we must make it so that they 'determine objects', which at present they do not. We must see to it that the terms 'substance', 'cause', etc., acquire an objective meaning, as opposed merely to a linguistic one —that they specify something about the character of things, not merely about the character of judgments-about-things. We must answer the question: What must something be like for it to be a substance, that is, for it to occupy a subject position in our thinking, for us to predicate things of it? (And what would 'predicate' mean objectively?) And: What must something be like to be a cause, that is for it to be 'something from which we can conclude to the existence of something else'? We need to know 'what sort of thing it is that demands one of these functions rather than another'. These are all ways of putting the question which the chapter on Schematism is designed to answer. Given the nature of the categories, as originally introduced, Kant's pursuit of this question is not only legitimate, but absolutely necessary if the categories are to have, as we know they must have, application to things. We know that they must apply, we do not know how they possibly can apply. They are not yet the kind of things of which it even makes good sense to say that they 'apply' to things. What the categories are altogether lacking, what they need to be supplied with, are criteria for their application. The schemata are just such criteria.

This is not, of course, the end of the matter as regards the legitimacy of the problem for Schematism. I imagine the following objection. The question of how the categories can have application may indeed be a legitimate, and even necessary, question *given* Kant's device of presenting the categories as unschematized in the first place. But there is no philosophical reason for this highly artificial procedure; no reason—other than perhaps some 'architectural' one—why the categories should not have been presented from the very start as what they eventually turn out to be, fully fledged concepts of things.[19]

This objection can be understood in two ways. Since Kant in fact derives the categories from the judgment forms, we can understand the objection to be saying either (a) Kant should have derived *schematized* categories from the judgment forms; or, if that is not possible or desirable, (b) he should have arrived at his list of fundamental concepts in some other way than by basing

[19] Bennett, *Kant's Analytic*, p. 151.

his account of them on the judgment forms. I shall deal with each of these in turn.

As regards (a), I am persuaded, with Kant, that no such derivation is possible. A schematized category, like any fully fledged concept, has vertical relations, it 'determines an object'. This means that it contains a description of an object not merely in linguistic terms—in terms of the role that the object's name plays in judgments—but in objective terms, that is, in terms of whatever manner it is in which objects are actually presented ('given') to us. Now, since—as shown in the Transcendental Aesthetic—objects can be presented to us only in space and time, this entails that the schematized category contains a description of an object in spatio-temporal terms.[20] Thus, for example, the schematized category *substance* is the concept of, contains the description of an object as, something which endures through changes in its states. I think it should be clear that there can be no way of immediately deriving such a concept, such a description in temporal terms, from the corresponding judgment form. In general, no examination of the function of unity in judgment, of the coherent-making operations of the understanding, can of itself yield any description of an object in spatial or temporal terms, or in terms of any other mode of access one might have to objects. To bring this point into sharper relief it is worth mentioning that there is no parallel obstacle to the derivation of the *un*schematized categories. For although we can say, if we wish, that the unschematized category *substance* 'describes an object'—namely as something-we-conceive-as-subject—that description in no way characterizes the thing in any terms in which objects can be present ('given') to us. We do not learn from this description anything about what the object will look like or feel like; we learn nothing, in short, about how it will appear to us, whatever the mode of appearance might be. Such a description does not 'determine an object'. But the

[20] An object does not of course have to exist to be 'determined'; the concept of a unicorn determines its object as fully as does the concept of a horse.

description contained in any *schematized* category does precisely that; and that is why the schematized categories cannot be derived from the judgment forms. There is no direct route from functions of unity to concepts of objects.

Let us therefore turn to the second version, (b), of the objection we are considering, namely that Kant should have arrived at his list of fundamental concepts in some other way than by basing his account of them on the judgment forms: if he had done so he would not have had the pseudo-problem of how the categories can have application to objects, the problem of Schematism.

This is a much larger issue than the one we have just dealt with, in (a). *Why*, we need to ask, does Kant base his account of concept-possession on the judgment forms, on the functions of unity in judgments? Could he have based his account on something else? We cannot begin to satisfy these queries until we have some idea of what the issue really is here. What is the question, what are the questions, to which an account of concept possession is meant to provide an answer? What is the basis of Kant's concern? It is not, I think, simply to arrive at an exhaustive list of fundamental and indispensable concepts. (Kant is not merely trying to do systematically what Aristotle, on his view, did haphazardly (See A81/B107).)

Kant's account of concept possession is, I believe, motivated and guided precisely by his recognition of what we have called the duality of concepts, by the realization that a concept is, or involves, two apparently different things: on the one hand it contains a 'function of unity', on the other hand it 'determines an object'. Let us quickly rehearse the issues here. To have understanding of anything, to possess any concept, say that of a dog, involves on the one hand being able to think coherently with the thought-element 'dog'—to fashion intelligible thought-structures, like 'The dog is black' (singular, affirmative, categorical, assertoric), not like 'The is dog black' (which set of representations lacks any functions of unity).[21] And on the other hand, it is to be able to apply the term 'dog' to objects in the world, that is in space and time. To have the concept 'dog', to understand anything by its means, requires both of these things. If one lacks the former, then one's intuitions of dogs, one's confrontations with them, are 'blind' (A51/B75): one cannot, as if in the dark, make anything out with regard to them, they mean nothing to one. If, on the other hand, one lacks the latter, the vertical ability, then one's thoughts are 'empty' (ibid.), no object is determined for one, those thoughts are about nothing at all.

Now, I think Kant's procedure, in those parts of the *Critique* we are considering, can best be seen as a response to this duality of concepts and to the philosophical question it poses. That question is this: How, given the dual nature of concept possession, are concepts of anything possible? How are we to *account* for the fact of concept possession, given that duality? Or, with a certain twist: What must the *source* of concepts be, in light of the fact that having a concept of anything has this dual nature? Kant's starting point in response to this issue is his conviction that none of the accounts of concept possession contained or implicit in the philosophies of his predecessors could be satisfactory. All of these earlier accounts, however different from one another in other ways, had this in common, that they explained the possession of concepts in terms, ultimately,[22] of intuition of objects (see e.g. Bxvi–xvii). Philosophers as diverse as Plato, Descartes, and Hume unquestioningly assumed that concepts derive from objects, that the source of concepts is acquaintance with things. Thus, it is acquaintance with the form of the dog (Plato), with dogs themselves, as the intellect sees them (Descartes), with the component sensory elements of

---

[21] I am here directly imagining a collection of representations which lacks the unity of a thought, and I am *illustrating* this with the ill-formed sentence. I am not, in other words, *inferring* the lack of unity from the fact that the words do not constitute a well-formed sentence in English.

[22] The explanation is not always direct, as, e.g. in the case of Locke's 'complex ideas'.

dog-perceptions (Hume), that accounts for our concept of a dog.

Now, I think this kind of account is not only natural and plausible, but inevitable *if* one pays more-or-less exclusive attention, as these philosophers did, to the second, the vertical aspect of concept possession. That concepts derive from objects will seem unquestionable so long as one sees the possession of a concept as something consisting primarily, if not solely, in the ability to apply that concept to that thing, in the ability, that is, to recognize or identify it as of a given kind. And it will seem unquestionable if, further, one forgets, or does not realize, that to apply a concept to something, to recognize or identify it as of a certain kind, is always to form a coherent thought ('This is . . .', 'That is . . .'), involving functions of the understanding.[23] It will seem unquestionable if one supposes that applying or recognizing or identifying consists simply in the mind's being confronted with something familiar (or what resembles something familiar), something of which (or of the prototype of which) one had previously formed an idea, a mental counterpart, and which is now seen to match that idea.

Kant rejects this picture of the nature and genesis of concepts *in toto*. The possession of concepts cannot be reduced to its applicational, vertical aspect. And there is no possibility, moreover, that confrontation with objects might somehow *generate* the functions of unity, the horizontal dimension. As regards the former, the functions of unity cannot be *ignored*, for without them no thought is possible at all—there could be no such thing as recognizing, as seeing or supposing anything to be anything; the mind would be no better than a camera. 'Intuitions without concepts are blind'; by themselves they do not make for perceptions at all. (The argument

---

[23] This is so even though there might be nothing in the mind, i.e. available to introspection, on a given occasion, but an isolated thought-element (say 'dog'). If the occurrence of that thought-element constitutes recognition it will still be the thought *that this is a dog*, and so will involve functions of the understanding.

for these claims occurs in the Transcendental Deduction, which will be our subject in Chapters 4 and 5.) And, as regards the latter, the functions of unity, the coherent-making operations, could not be *derived* from objects. No confrontations with dogs, however forceful and lively and frequently repeated, could show that the only way to think of dogs is as things that subsist and in which things inhere—that 'the dog is black' is a possible thought, that 'the is dog black' is not. Nor can we suppose, as Descartes seems to have done, that our capacity to think of dogs in this way is made possible by an intellectual perception of canine essence. We are not equipped with such perceptual powers.

Now, whatever might be the merits of Kant's case here —we shall discuss this in detail later—it is clear, given his convictions, that he could not follow his predecessors in supposing that concepts derive from objects. But what alternatives to that traditional approach are there? Whatever account one proposes, it must give due prominence to *both* aspects of concept-possession, the horizontal and the vertical, if we are to avoid, as we surely must, both blind intuitions and empty thought-structures as the product of our account. It seems clear from his treatment of the issues that Kant believed that the only way to account for both of these aspects was to *bifurcate the account itself*, to give a two-pronged explanation of how concepts of things are possible. He supposed—we shall see later whether rightly—that there is no single, monolithic account that could take care of both the functions of unity and the determining of objects at once. And this seems, initially at least, plausible enough: one has to start one's account with one or the other of the two aspects; there seems to be no vantage point from which one could take both into consideration at once. Now, we know that we cannot begin with the vertical aspect, with objects. That will end where it begins, in a blind alley; there is no possible transition from there to the understanding of anything. The only alternative, it seems, is to start with the functions of unity. These, though mere thought-structures and in themselves quite incapable of having application, seem to have at least this advantage over their competitor as a potential starting point for an account, that one can add to them, and thereby, by stages, create the requisite product, a concept of something. Whereas there is no route from blind, unseeing confrontation with things to the understanding of things, there is, Kant hoped, a route to that goal from the structure of the understanding itself.

I have tried here to explain why it is that Kant finds it necessary to base his account of concept possession on the judgment forms, the functions of unity. Given the duality of concepts on the one hand, and his critique of traditional accounts on the other, there seems to be no easy alternative to the procedure he adopts. And given that procedure, the derivation of the categories from the judgment forms, the question as to how the categories can find application, can 'determine objects' is, as I argued earlier, a genuine question. It is not enough to 'have' categories, logical functions for bringing the manifold under a concept; we also need to know 'what sort of thing it is that demands one of these functions rather than another'.

So we must provide the understanding with its vertical dimension, the categories with schemata, criteria for their application to things in the world.

The question is, can that be done? I do not mean merely, is Kant's actual schematization of the categories successful? (It consists in appending to each category a time-predicate, *eine Zeitbestimmung*.) My question has a more general scope. Is it possible to schematize the categories at all? Is there, in other words, any route whatever from functions of unity to concepts of objects? I believe there is not. And the reason is this. If, as Kant maintains, the categories are merely the functions of unity conceived as having verticality, as ranging over possible objects of thought, then there is no way of arriving at criteria for their application to things but by picking those criteria out of a hat. If the category-terms 'substance', 'cause', 'totality' have in their original state only 'linguistic' meaning, if they are quite uninformative as to the nature of the objects to which they will eventually, when schematized, apply—then the only way they can be given 'objective' meaning, be made descriptive of objects, is an utterly arbitrary way. If 'substance' there means no more than 'a something-conceived-only-as-subject . . .', and if that in itself does not tell us what *in the world* a substance is, then there is nothing in it that points to, or even suggests, one criterion for its application rather than another. There is no reason at all why permanence in time, rather than, say, non-existence at any time, should be the time-predicate that characterizes those things we conceive as subjects. One cannot discover, one can only blindly stipulate 'what sort of thing it is that demands one of these functions rather than another'. Nothing could count as an argument to the effect that a given schema, and no other, goes with a given category. And in fact, Kant does not attempt to argue: he simply announces the schemata seriatim, in the order of the categories (A142/B181–A145/B184).

Now, one cannot avoid this issue of arbitrariness by supposing the application criteria to be empirical—by delegating the job of schematizing the categories to experience. For the situation there is the same: someone armed with only unschematized categories could have no more reason for regarding any one kind of thing presented to him rather than any other kind of thing as 'subject only'. Kant was right in insisting that the schemata would have to be a priori as much as the categories themselves are a priori; they would have to be built right into the understanding itself, into our capacity to conceive things at all. The difficulty consists in seeing *how* they can be built in.

It is only, I think, if one surreptitiously keeps in the back of one's mind at least part of the 'objective' meaning, the descriptive force, of the category terms ('substance', etc.) that it can seem natural and reasonable to assign them these and these application criteria rather than others. It is only if we allow ourselves a sidelong glance at the 'objective', the in-the-world employment of subject-predicate sentences that it will be reasonable to say that the things we think of as subjects are permanent things, things that endure through changes in their states. But such sidelong glances are not permitted in this enterprise of Kant's. To permit them is to beg the question as to how the categories are to be schematized, and to do that is to make it impossible to have derived the categories from the judgment forms in the first place. For if one can see in the category what the criterion for its application would be, then the category is no longer a mere logical form for a concept of something; it already 'determines an object', has descriptive force. But then it cannot, as we saw earlier, be derived from the corresponding judgment form. If, on the other hand, the category *can* be derived from the judgment form, then matching a given schema to it can be nothing but a quite arbitrary act. Kant seems not to have noticed this awkward dilemma.

But why should it matter, I can imagine someone asking, that the assignment of schemata to the categories is arbitrary? Indeed, isn't this just what one would expect? Anything else would be, as we have just pointed out, question-begging, and would make the metaphysical deduction of the categories impossible. The very fact that Kant finds it necessary, as we showed above, to give a two-pronged explanation of how concepts of things are possible makes it inevitable, surely, that the schemata have a source quite different from that of the categories, and so makes it inevitable that the conjoining of the one to the other will seem arbitrary.

I think this is true; the situation is inevitable, given Kant's starting-point and his concerns. But that does not mean that the arbitrariness of the connection of schema to category is acceptable. I believe in fact that that arbitrariness destroys the very integrity of what it is to have a concept of something. An account of what it is to possess concepts of things must not only allow for the duality of concepts and give due prominence to each of the two aspects involved, it must also specify those aspects in such a way that we can see *how* they belong together; it is not enough to be told *that* they do so. An explanation of what it is to have the concept of a dog, for example, must specify the horizontal aspect, the functions of unity, the operations requisite for forming coherent thoughts with the thought-element 'dog'; it must also specify the vertical aspect, the spatio-temporal criteria for the application of the term to things in the world. But it must specify these in such a way as to enable us to see that the criteria *fit*, that they are *the right ones* for those functions of unity. This is not one of those places where explanations must come to an end; the explanation fails if it allows that any other criteria would have done just as well, that no criterion is any more fitting for a given logical function than any other. The fact that having a concept of something is a dual capacity must not permit us to make of it a hybrid of two unconnectable elements. It must not be made to seem sheer happenstance, something completely unaccountable, that our regarding dogs as enduring through changes in their states should go together with our predicating things of them in our thoughts, rather than with our performing some quite different thought-operation. We cannot, I submit, make any sense of the idea that enduring-through-changes-in-states might just as well have been the schema of, say, cause, rather than of substance; or, conversely, that the criterion for something's being conceived as subject might have been regular succession (which is in fact the schema of causality), rather than permanence. Kant's account cannot throw any light on the fact that these are not possibilities for us, for there is no way open to him of demonstrating the connection of category and schema; no way, that is, of articulating the *unity* of a concept. And so his account must fail; he cannot in the end show how concepts of things are possible.

Kant was aware, I believe, of his failure to demonstrate the connection of schema to category, and he attributed the failure to the nature of the case, as if to say 'the explanation comes to an end here': 'This schematism of our understanding . . . is an art concealed in the depths of the human soul, whose real modes of activity nature is hardly likely ever to allow us to discover, and to have open to our gaze' (A141–/B180–1). To discover the real modes of activity of Schematism would be to have open to our gaze the conceptual mechanism that connects this schema to this category, and that to that, and allows no room for alternative connections. I think the device of relegating the mechanism to a secret place hides from Kant the realization that his failure to show how the connection between category and schema works means that his account of concept possession itself must fail. And this is indeed what it means. It means that the final link in the chain, the one that should at last fasten the machinery of the understanding on to objects in space and time, eludes him.

Now, this failure of Kant's account leaves us with a major problem on our hands. For it is clear from the argument above that his inability to show how the categories can find (non-arbitrary) application to things in the world has deep roots in his theory of the nature of the human understanding. This inability is the immediate result, I think, of his belief that only a bifurcated, a two-pronged explanation of how concepts of things are possible could do justice to the dual nature of concepts. It is the result of his belief that only an account starting from two quite unrelated points could explain how it is that a concept involves both functions of unity and determinations of objects in spatio-temporal terms. And that belief, that only a two-pronged explanation could work, is itself forced upon him, it seems, by his conviction that the two aspects of the duality are independent of each other, that neither can be derived from or reduced to the other.

Now, if we find this last consideration a plausible one —if we feel that there is something right about the idea that concepts have a dual nature, and that neither of the component aspects is reducible to the other—then we inherit for ourselves the problem of how concepts of things are possible. And that problem, at this stage of our inquiry, becomes this: How are we to provide a unified, an undivided, explanation of concept possession, an explanation which, while giving due prominence to both aspects of the duality, nevertheless proceeds from a single point? That, I propose, is what a successful account of concept possession would have to be like. I think Kant was darkly groping at the idea of a unified account when he wondered whether sensibility and understanding 'perhaps spring from a common, but to us unknown, root' (A15/B29). Chapter 3 will examine the question of whether such an account is possible.

3

A Reconsideration

So we are faced once more with Kant's question: How, given the dual nature of concept possession, are concepts of things possible? More specifically, in the light of what we have learned from Kant's failure to answer that question satisfactorily: How, given the apparently irreducible duality of concept possession, are we to account for its integrity? How are we to make sense of the fact that having a concept of something is an indivisible, unitary capacity when, after all, concept possession has a dual nature? What kind of story of what concept possession consists in will do justice to these apparently conflicting considerations? The kind of account we need, I think, will be one that portrays concept possession as a *single* capacity and the two aspects of the duality as, in some way, *abstractions* from that single capacity. What would that sort of account be like?

But before we confront these issues directly, a number of prior considerations will need to be met. Is it really true, outside the framework of Kant's philosophy, that concepts have a dual nature in the relevant sense? What would the component aspects consist in? Can we, above all, accept the idea that a concept is a 'function of the understanding', a 'function of unity' as well as that it 'determines objects'? We will need to examine that idea of duality in a fresh way, unencumbered by Kant's machinery.

Now, if the guiding idea behind that of functions of unity is the idea of logical form, then the whole business of duality may turn out to be a fiction. For, it will be said, we now know something which Kant did not know, namely that there are no indispensable logical forms.

Strawson, for example, claims, '. . . the logician can, if he chooses, distinguish indefinitely many forms of proposition, all belonging to formal logic' and '. . . as far as logical forms are concerned, the logician's choice of primitives *is* a choice'.[1] Bennett goes a stage further: the very idea of formality, understood in an unqualified sense, is suspect. '. . . the form/content distinction is not absolute but relative . . . relative to the judgment-features which have been intensively studied in what are called "formal" systems of logic'.[2] (And he imagines developments in logic which would result in the inclusion among forms terms like 'most' (as well as 'all'), 'is evidence for' (as well as 'entails'), 'is similar to' (as well as 'is identical with'), and so on.)

If there are no indispensable logical forms, or—worse still perhaps—if there is no such thing, 'absolutely', as the logical form of a judgment, what can be left of the idea of functions of unity (or functions of the understanding, moments of thought)? Isn't the idea of logical form basic here? Don't these claims of Strawson's and Bennett's undermine Kant's strategy altogether? I do not think that they do. For it does not follow from these claims about logical form that there is no such thing as the '*unity*', or *coherence*, of a thought. There will still be a difference, if there was one in the first place, between those aggregations of thought-elements that constitute a thought—that have the requisite unity or coherence— and those that do not. What has to be discarded, if Strawson's or Bennett's claims are true, is not the idea of the unity of a thought as such, but, rather, what Kant took to be his 'Clue' for the means whereby such unity is achieved—for identifying the functions or operations of unity. If Strawson or Bennett is right, formal logic cannot do this job. That does not mean that there is no job to be done.

But this may seem only to postpone the undermining of our hopes of preserving the idea of functions of unity.

---

[1] P. F. Strawson, *The Bounds of Sense* (London, 1966), 79, 80.
[2] Jonathan Bennett, *Kant's Analytic* (Cambridge, 1966), 80.

For, it will be said, if formal logic cannot tell us what these functions are, then, surely, nothing can tell us what they are *for thought in general*. If logic does not contain the rules for thinking-in-general, for forming a thought quite irrespective of all subject matter, then nothing does. This seems right. But I think the idea of functions of unity, of a horizontal dimension to thinking, can survive even this blow. Something again has to be discarded. This time it is the idea that there is a *single* set of functions of unity (the Table of Categories) for *all* concepts, for thinking about *any* possible object. But that does not prevent us from entertaining the possibility of there being functions of unity which are peculiar to given concepts or groups of concepts. The idea would be this. Though there may be no rules for thinking in general (the judgment forms), and therefore no rules for thinking about anything you please (the categories)—there may nevertheless be rules for thinking about such things as *dogs*, other rules for thinking about such things as *pains*, others again for *games*, for *storms*, for *explanations*, for *money*, and so on.

Kant did not entertain the possibility of such particularized rules. He firmly believed that the requisite operations of the understanding for thinking about any one kind of thing are the same as those for thinking about anything else. And he had powerful reasons for believing this. The only way, he would have said, of arriving at functions of unity, at coherent-making operations of the mind, is by abstracting from all differences among the objects of thought. Why? Because, he thought, such differences can be taken into account only by attending to what actual intuition, actual confrontation with objects, tells us about those objects. Only intuition can distinguish one kind of object of thought from another. But to allow intuition to enter the picture at this point would be to put the cart before the horse. We are interested, after all, in how we must think about things if we are to be conscious of them at all, if we are not to be 'blind' in their presence. To now be told that to determine how we must think about them if we are not to be blind to them we must take into account how they strike us while still blind to them is clearly not helpful. If the functions of unity are to enable us to be conscious of objects, they cannot depend upon any preview, any prior awareness, of what those objects look like to us.

Now I think Kant is right on this last point. The findings of intuition cannot be allowed to play any role in the functions of unity. That is to say, how things appear to us cannot form any part of the conditions for thinking coherently about them in the first place. For we can be aware of things as appearing thus and so only given that we can already think about them coherently.

But I do not think Kant is right in believing that only intuition can enable us to mark differences among objects of thought. We can, as we shall see later, distinguish from one another such things as dogs and headaches and explanations *as objects of thought*, without taking into account any observational differences among such objects. Or, to put the point another way, we can distinguish the concept of a headache from the concept of a dog, the meaning of the word 'headache' from the meaning of the word 'dog', without resorting to observationally acquired facts about what the objects of these concepts are respectively like. If this is correct, then the idea of functions of unity, of a horizontal dimension to concepts, can survive the objection we considered earlier about logical form. There will be no one set of functions of unity for all possible concepts; instead they will vary from one kind of concept to another.

But my purpose in putting forward this idea of particularized functions of unity is not simply, of course, to evade that objection about logical form. I believe, in fact, that it is only in particularized form, only in relation to given concepts, or groups of concepts, that there exists such a thing at all as a horizontal dimension to thinking. Kant was mistaken in taking the logical form of propositions as his 'clue' for the functions of unity not only because there is no such thing 'absolutely' as logical form. He would have been mistaken in his procedure even if there had been such a thing. For logical form is, even if necessary, in any case quite insufficient for the coherence of a thought. A string of words may incorporate the requisite forms of quantity, quality, relation, and modality and still fail to unite its elements into the expression of a thought. The sentence 'The explanation above her left eye throbbed so violently that she had to bite her lip to keep from screaming' satisfies all these formal requirements but fails to say anything coherent with the thought-element 'explanation'.[3] It does not succeed in uniting that element in an intelligible way with those that adjoin it. 'Explanation' and 'pain', though both substance-words and so belonging to the same Kantian category, do not have the same 'logic'; they have different horizontal settings. (And the settings for 'dog' and 'money' and 'storm' are of course different again.)

With this in mind, let us now tentatively reformulate the duality of concept possession in a general way, without restriction to the specifics of Kant's philosophy. I propose the following: Someone who has a given concept, say that of a dog, is (a) able to form coherent thoughts with the thought-element 'dog'. That is, he is able to think such things as 'Take that dog away', 'The dog ate all the meat', 'There's a dog under my bed'. And (b) he is able to apply the thought-element 'dog' appropriately to things in the world. That is, among other things, he is able to recognize the bearing that certain states of affairs have on the propositions in (a). He knows the relevance, for example, to the last of the three propositions cited there, of there being—visibly and tangibly to him—nothing at all under his bed. (It is not enough to know the relevance to that proposition of the *proposition* 'There is nothing under the bed'; see note 9 to Chapter 2.) He must in a practical sense know what sort of thing counts as there being a dog under his bed.

I think it is clear that we could devise similar

---

[3] This is not to say that such a form of words could under no circumstances make sense; it is to say that without further ado, given how we in fact use the term 'explanation', it makes no sense. And the same, *mutatis mutandis*, is true of the form of words 'The is dog black'.

formulations of duality for other and quite different concepts than that of a dog.

It should be noted before we go further that our duality does not depend in any way on any peculiarities of the terminology of 'concept' or of 'having concepts'. We can accommodate those who, like Warnock, find these terms too psychologistic and prefer instead to talk of 'the use of words'. We can allow, as Warnock has it, that ' "I have the concept of whiteness" means the same as "I know how to use 'white' " '.[4] For the use of a word, in the relevant sense of that phrase, has precisely the same two dimensions or aspects as does the concept. We can, that is to say, express our duality as follows. To have mastery of the use of the word 'dog' involves being able both (a) to use the word 'dog' *in* coherent, intelligible locutions. It is to be able to say such things as . . ., etc;—and (b) to apply the word appropriately to, use the word appropriately *of*, things in the world . . . . Whether we talk of concepts or of uses of words we will have the same horizontal and vertical dimensions. Sometimes it is more convenient and, as we shall see, even enlightening, to talk of uses of words, and I shall henceforth often do so. It is also sometimes dangerous to talk in this way. One risks being understood, and understanding oneself, as making some parochial and reductionistic point about the standard employment of some English word. In so far as our two dimensions are dimensions of the use of words, they are so by, and only by, being dimensions of *thinking*, *understanding*, *meaning* anything *by* those words.

We have now put forward a general formulation of the duality of concept possession, one that is independent of Kant's system, and we should pause here to remind ourselves of our larger aims. The goal of the present chapter is to see whether we can give an account of concept possession which, unlike Kant's, does justice both to the fact that it has a dual nature, and also to the fact that it has an essential unity or integrity. Our main question is: What kind of characterization of the capacity

---

[4] G. J. Warnock, 'Concepts and Schematism', *Analysis* (1949), 78.

called concept possession will make it plain that that capacity is, despite its dual nature, after all a unitary thing and not a merely arbitrary conjunction of two quite discrete capacities? We cannot immediately push ahead with this inquiry, however. We need to satisfy ourselves first that the duality in our formulation is genuine, that is, that having a concept requires both of these components.

In individual cases, it might seem (as it does to Chipman, see note 4 to Chapter 2) that the horizontal component is of itself sufficient for concept possession. We might well allow that someone has the concept of bone-marrow or of a tadpole if he employs these words coherently in locutions, even though he has little or no idea what these things look like. This will be particularly so if, in the one case, he knows, is able to say, that bone-marrow has something to do with bones, and is able to recognize bones; and if, in the other case, he knows, is able to say, that tadpoles are small animate things, and is able to recognize other animate things. In short, we might allow someone certain concepts on the strength of horizontal mastery alone, so long as he can relate those concepts to others which he possesses in a fully fledged way. But it should be clear that horizontal mastery is by no means sufficient in general. A person who although (miraculously perhaps) perfectly able to form all sorts of coherent sentences, completely lacked the ability to apply any of his words vertically, to things in the world, would not have a *language* at all. In uttering his well-formed sentences he would not be expressing thoughts about, or to the effect that, anything whatever. His thoughts would be empty thought-structures, his stock of utterances would be like a parrot's repertoire.

It is perhaps less obvious that the vertical capacity is also by itself insufficient for concept possession. The reason that it is less obvious, I think, is this. It seems reasonable to say that it is sufficient for having the concept of a dog that one be able to recognize dogs, to apply the word, or thought-element, 'dog' to whatever is a dog. Someone who can say or think 'dog' when, and only when, confronted with a member of that species surely has the concept, or at least *a* rudimentary concept, of a dog. He has at least some, indeed a central, understanding of what 'dog' means. I think this is true. But the reason it is true is that this sort of talk does not in fact confine itself exclusively to the vertical component. For, in this context, to say or think 'dog' when confronted with a dog, to recognize something as a dog, can only be to say or think *that this is a dog*. The occurrence of the thought-element 'dog' already has here the force of a thought; and only someone capable of forming coherent thoughts with that thought-element can give it that force. That someone utters the word 'dog' in the presence of dogs shows us that he has the concept of a dog because, and only because, we, quite justifiably, take it that he is *calling* these things dogs, expressing the thought that they are dogs. If, however, *ex hypothesi*, he lacks the horizontal capacity to form (coherent) thoughts of this kind, then his behaviour does not show at all that he has the concept of a dog.

What we have been saying here raises a certain important issue about the horizontal component of concept possession which, though we noted it earlier (see note 23 to Chapter 2), has not been emphasized hitherto. An intelligible locution might on occasion consist of only one word, like the utterance 'dog' used in the example above to express recognition. Equally, a coherent thought might sometimes, for all I know, consist in the occurrence of a single thought-element. We are not in a position to deny this possibility, nor would such a denial be to the point. The question of whether something is a coherent thought is not ultimately the question of whether its several elements are combined in a certain way, as Kant seems to have supposed. It is, rather, the question of whether the occurrence of those elements (or on occasion that element) has, as we have put it, a certain *force*. A sufficient test for its having such a force will be whether or not there is a coherent English sentence that expresses it; and what force it has will be shown by what sentence that is. Thus, to see that the occurrence of the thought-element 'dog', in the example above, has the force of the thought that this is a dog it is sufficient to see that that occurrence can be expressed by the sentence 'This is a dog'.

It is clear, then, that neither of the constituent capacities of concept possession, the horizontal and the vertical, is, in isolation, sufficient for having the concept of something. Both are necessary; and our duality is to that extent a genuine one. If one is to have the concept of a dog (or of an explanation), one must be able both to think coherently with the thought-element 'dog' ('explanation'), and, *ceteris paribus*, to recognize things in the world as dogs (explanations).

Now Kant, faced with this duality, found it necessary, as we saw, to bifurcate his account of concept possession, to give a two-pronged explanation of how concepts of things are possible. He could not find a single, undivided, characterization of what it is to have concepts of things, that could embrace the horizontal and the vertical capacity at once. He could not see *how* it is that whatever enables us to form coherent thoughts could also provide us with criteria for the application of those thoughts. For, as he saw clearly, on the one hand, the coherent-making operations of the mind cannot of themselves 'determine objects'; and, on the other hand, mere intuition of objects cannot explain our capacity to form coherent thoughts about them.

On this last point Kant was right. Neither of the two constituents of concept possession contains the other, they are distinct components; both are individually necessary for having the concept of something. But it may nevertheless be the case that there is some higher, or broader, characterization of concept possession which embraces *both* components. I believe a 'higher' characterization of this kind can be found in, or extrapolated from, Wittgenstein's notion of a language-game.[5]

Wittgenstein, like Warnock, holds that to have concepts is to know, to have mastery of, the use of words.

[5] See in particular *Philosophical Investigations*, 2nd edn. (Oxford, 1967), *passim*.

But he talks about what it is to have mastery of the use of words in such a way as to enable us to see that that mastery is not merely a horizontal capacity, nor merely a vertical capacity, *nor* a mere conjunction of the two, but that it is an integrated ability, from which our two constituent capacities can be seen as abstractions. To have concepts, to have mastered the use of words, is, for Wittgenstein, to be capable of participating in certain kinds of activities, which he calls 'language-games'; it is to be able to perform certain kinds of actions, 'moves' in language-games, which involve the utterance of the words in question. Thus, for example, to have the concept of a slab or a block is to be able to do such things as ask someone to bring or take away a slab or a block, and to be able to respond appropriately to someone else's request to do such a thing. It is to be able to utter the word 'slab' or 'block' in the context of, or with the force of, such requests, and to be able to respond appropriately to such utterances on the part of others. This example, taken from the early paragraphs of the *Investigations* (§§2–20), is of course enormously oversimplified—that is what Wittgenstein means when he calls it a 'primitive form of language' (§5). Asking someone to fetch and deliver is only one of an indefinite number of kinds of action the ability to perform which epitomizes mastery of the use of words like 'slab' and 'block'. But the simplicity of the example does not take away from its point. To have the concept of a slab is to be able to do such things as make and follow requests for slabs. To have mastered the use of a word is to be in a position to behave in certain recognized ways with the word, it is to be able, in practice, to give the word its 'role' or 'place' in human activities. And this is a quite general point. It holds as much for the concepts 'pain' or 'between' or 'red' or 'explanation', as it does for 'slab'.

Now, and this is the crucial step for our purposes, to be able, in practice, to give a word its role or place in human activities is not merely to be able to give it its (horizontal) position in sentences. Nor is it to be able to do this and also to be able to associate the word (vertically) with some spatio-temporal correspondent, its referent. The ability to make a move in a language-game is not a composite of two, initially and metaphysically separate, abilities. It can be seen to involve these two sub-abilities without being thereby regarded as a construct out of them. Someone who can employ the word 'slab' in the language-game will use the word intelligibly in sentences.[6] He will say such things as 'Put that slab there, next to the block', not things like 'The slab returns as a wistful echo after the cadenza'. And he will also, for example, and other things being equal, pick up and put down slabs when called upon to do so—showing that he recognizes things in the world as slabs. But these two aspects or dimensions of the use of a word go hand in hand from the beginning; we learn them together when we learn the language, when we are 'trained' to perform these and those actions. There are, indeed, not two things to learn, only one: how to use the word in the performance of these acts. It is only in retrospect that we can see a duality in this unitary thing.

If this is so, then there is no need, as there is with Kant, to bring the conceptual machinery to that foreign place, the world, and to try, vainly, to doctor it in such a way as to make it fit the world, make it 'homogeneous' with it. Whereas the ability to put together sentences according to logical form does have to be connected to the world, being by itself 'without application', the ability to use words in the language-game is already in the world. The use of the word 'slab' in activities like making and responding to requests does not have to be brought into relation with slabs—it already deals directly with them. The functions of unity, the operations of the understanding, are in the language-game already schematized.

Now it might be thought that we have succeeded in

---

[6] This holds for 'advanced' languages, like English and German, in which a structural distinction between words and sentences exists. It does not hold for the primitive language which Wittgenstein imagines in §§2–20 of the *Investigations*. One of Wittgenstein's purposes in introducing this 'primitive' case is precisely to turn us away from the idea (in Kant, Russell, and others) that the well-formed sentence is crucial and basic to the nature of language. It is the 'role' of the sentence, the work it does in the language-game, that is the important and basic thing.

reaching this conclusion only by sacrificing what Kant took to be an essential ingredient in the operations of the understanding, namely their 'purity', their independence from everything empirical, from all data of intuition. 'Of course,' I can imagine someone saying, 'if you focus upon those activities in which we deal with actual things in the world, then you will have no problem about relating those activities to those things. But then you will have failed to do what Kant rightly insisted one do—abstract from all intuition of objects.'

It is true that if the capacity to engage in language-games is to play the Kantian role we wish it to play—if it is to contain the operations of the understanding without which we could not conceive anything at all—then that capacity must have the same 'purity' that Kant insisted upon for his schematized categories.[7] If mastery of the language-game with the word 'slab' is to be the *sine qua non* of our being conscious of such things as slabs, then it cannot depend upon prior observational knowledge of what slabs are like.

But I do not believe that the capacity to engage in the language-game does depend upon any prior observational knowledge of its object. What might make it look as if it does is the fact that there are, inferable from the sense of utterances in the language-game, propositions which seem to express truths about the object. Thus, from the use of the words 'slab', 'pain', 'explanation', in their respective language-games, we can infer that slabs are solid things that are picked up and put down, but are not expressed in human behaviour; with pains the converse is true; pains, again, are located, for example above the left eye, explanations are not; and they, unlike both slabs and pains, are ill-advised, consistent, or hasty.

Now it might seem that we must know, or at least believe, these propositions about slabs, pains, and explanations to be true if we are to engage in the respective language-games. How could we ask someone to bring us

---

[7] It must be remembered that the schematized category, as well as the unschematized, owes nothing to intuition of objects, contains nothing empirical. What the schema adds to the category is a feature of the *form* of sensible intuition; it adds nothing which results from actual intuition.

a slab if we did not already believe that slabs can be picked up? How could we comfort him when he writhes and moans if we did not believe that pains are expressed in behaviour? How could we criticize him for his hasty explanation if we did not know that explanations are the sorts of things that can be hasty? And our knowledge or belief that these things are true must surely, it will seem, be based on some kind of acquaintance with, observation of, their respective objects.

I think this is an illusion. It does not follow from the fact that these propositions can be inferred from the moves of the language-game that therefore one's capacity (or preparedness) to engage in the language-game depends upon their prior acceptance. I believe that these propositions have in fact the same status as the proposition 'dogs endure through changes in their states', understood as we have understood it through Kant. Here too it might seem that our capacity to think of dogs in the way in which, on Kant's view, we do think of them, depends upon a prior acceptance of this proposition. That is, it might seem that our categorizing dogs as substances depends upon a prior intuitional recognition of this truth about them. But it is clear that that 'truth', far from *underlying* our categorization of dogs, does no more than *record the fact* that this is indeed how we do categorize them. It records the fact that dogs are thought as subjects of predicates, and that whatever, in space and time, is thought as a subject of predicates is thereby thought as enduring through changes in its states. That is all there is to the truth of this proposition. It owes nothing to the data of intuition, to any pre-conceptual awareness of what dogs are like. Call it a 'truth about dogs' if you like; it is so only because it is a truth about how we operate with the term 'dog', about what kind of concept 'dog' is.

Now, I maintain that the same holds for our propositions above 'about' slabs, pains, and explanations. To say that slabs, unlike pains, can be picked up and brought; that pains, unlike explanations, can be located above the eye, etc.—where these propositions are inferred from the sense of locutions employing these words—is simply to state what does and does not count as a move in the language-game. It is not as if pains had, on inspection, been found to be too delicate, or too flimsy, too much lacking in adhesiveness of parts, to be lifted by hand— whereas slabs had been found to be well suited to such treatment. Rather, it is that the utterance: 'Fetch that pain; put it on the mantelpiece, lean it against the wall' does not, as things stand, constitute an intelligible manœuvre with words; whereas the utterance 'Fetch that slab . . .' does. 'Slabs can be picked up', like 'Dogs endure . . .' is what Wittgenstein calls a 'grammatical' proposition; it tells us no more than how these words are intelligibly employed.

The qualification above, 'where these propositions are inferred from the sense of locutions employing these words' is crucial. It is only in so far as we regard the proposition in question (e.g. 'Slabs can be picked up') as having to be true given the sense of utterances (like 'Fetch that slab') which occur in the language-game with the word ('slab') that the proposition will be a grammatical one. No proposition is, as it were, *of itself* grammatical. Where, for instance, the contrast with slabs is not pains or explanations but, say, houses, then the situation is quite different. To say 'Slabs can be picked up' (houses can't) is to say something about human strength, nothing about how words are used in the language-game. (There is nothing in the use of the word 'house' that precludes the *intelligibility* of the request 'Bring me that house, put it there . . .'. We know what would count as complying with that request (compare 'Bring me that pain . . .'), even though we might have no idea as to what means to employ in trying to get the thing done.)

We must also be careful not to confuse those propositions which follow from what makes sense in the language-game (which propositions are, I am maintaining, invariably grammatical) with other propositions which can be inferred from the existence of the language-game itself. From the fact, for example, that there exists the language-game with the word 'slab' it can be inferred that some things can be moved by human agency from one place to another; that not everything is immovably fastened to the ground or unchangeably fluid; that human beings have sufficient bodily strength to lift some of these things, etc., etc. These are empirical propositions; they express what Wittgenstein calls 'very general facts of nature'.[8] Such facts underlie the language-game, in the sense that it is causally dependent on them; if they were to alter tomorrow, we would no longer be able to use the word 'slab' as we now use it. It is important to see, however, that these general facts of nature cannot distinguish any one kind of object of thought (e.g. a slab) from any other (e.g. an explanation). That there are solid, pick-up-able things in the world, a general fact, does not tell us what sorts of thing can (coherently) be picked up. 'Slabs can be picked up, explanations can't' does not express a fact of nature; it is not a pre-condition of our having the language-game, it can be inferred only from the sense of the locutions which constitute the moves of that language-game.

Now my main claim here is that any proposition which appears to be about an object of a given kind, and which can be inferred (solely) from the sense of the locutions which employ the word for the object—that such a proposition is invariably a grammatical one. It records merely how the word is used in the language-game; it does not express any underlying, intuitionally acquired insight into the nature of the object. This claim is grounded in the same way as, and is as plausible as, the parallel claim, implicit in Kant, that any proposition deducible from the way in which we categorize things (say dogs) records only how we think about those things, and does not express any preconceptual intuition of what they are like. Our thesis is the same as Kant's. The sense, the intelligibility, of utterances, the 'unity of thought' in what we say, is not based on any facts about objects.

So the objection made a few pages back has been answered. In our talk about the use of the word in the language-game, about how a word is coherently em-

---

[8] Wittgenstein, *Philosophical Investigations*, p. 230.

ployed, we are as capable of abstracting from all data of intuition as was Kant in his talk about schematized categories.

The argument of the present chapter is now in outline complete. I have tried to show that Wittgenstein's notion of a language-game can provide us with a key to the solution to Kant's intractable problem of how concepts of objects are possible. Kant could not solve his problem because he was obliged to regard the two aspects or dimensions of concept possession as having quite separate origins. He was unable to see how there could be one thing, one unpartitioned 'faculty', that contains both the coherent-making operations of the understanding in the possession of a concept and its determining of objects. All he could do was deal with each aspect separately—as if it were (though he knew otherwise) a distinct capacity —and then clamp them together by fiat.

The idea of mastery of a language-game is still a sketchy and hazy idea, and we have not, yet, done very much to clarify it. It is an issue which we will explore more fully, and in a larger context, in Chapter 6. But I hope that what has been said so far already enables one to see that such mastery *can* in principle amount to what Kant could not find, that single, unpartitioned capacity which constitutes concept possession and of which our two aspects can be seen *as* aspects. For the language-game not only contains the function of the understanding on the one hand, and the criterion for its application on the other; it also connects them. Whereas Kant could not but make it seem an arbitrary stipulation that a given criterion goes together with a given function of unity, the language-game shows how the two go together. Given the language-game we play with the word 'slab', in which, in certain circumstances, we say things like 'Bring that slab, put it there', it is no surprise that solidity, pick-up-ability, rather than, say moaning or writhing, should be a criterion of the word's application. Given the language-game with the word 'pain', in which, in certain situations, we say things like 'It will be better soon', it is no surprise that moaning and writhing, rather than, say, solidity, should be a criterion of pain. The Schematism of our understanding need no longer be regarded as a concealed art; it is open to our gaze. If all this is correct, then our practical mastery of the language, our capacity to use words in the world, could be the 'common root' which Kant despaired of finding. It could itself be that unitary capacity the exercise of which, at one stroke, makes our concepts sensible and our intuitions intelligible (A51/B75). But this is, so far, only a sketch. A fuller discussion of these issues must wait until we have seen further into Kant's attempt to explicate the nature of the understanding.

4

The Idea of a Transcendental Deduction ·

In our discussion of Kant's account of the nature of the understanding I have so far limited our focus to two non-contiguous sections of the *Critique*, the Clue to the Discovery of All Pure Concepts of the Understanding on the one hand—where Kant derives the categories from the judgment forms—and the chapter on the Schematism of the categories on the other. Lodged in between these two sections is that dense and difficult argument, the Transcendental Deduction of the Categories. We need to inquire about the role of this argument in the overall scheme. In particular I want to ask two kinds of questions. First, is there something lacking in the account of concept possession we have considered so far, something which the Transcendental Deduction is supposed to supply? Does the talk about unschematized categories on the one hand and their application criteria on the other leave a gap which the Transcendental Deduction is designed to fill? Secondly, (supposing that the Deduction does indeed play a role in Kant's account) does this role survive the transformation we proposed in Chapter 3 above? In other words, is the need for a Transcendental Deduction due merely to the unfortunate fact that Kant's account of concept possession proceeds from two unrelated points, or will there still be the need for such an argument once we have seen that concept possession is a unified, unpartitioned capacity? Does the Deduction address itself to a real issue, or merely to one that is artificially brought into being by the special needs of Kant's theory?

But before we pursue these questions, we should look briefly at Kant's own claims as to the purpose of the Deduction. Here are some characteristic formulations. I have numbered them for convenience.

1. ' . . . we are faced by the problem how these concepts [the categories] can relate to objects, when they are nevertheless not derived from any experience of objects.[1] The explanation of the manner in which concepts can thus relate a priori to objects I entitle their transcendental deduction . . .' (A85/B117).

2. 'Thus a difficulty such as we did not meet with in the field of sensibility is here presented, namely, how *subjective conditions of thought* can have *objective validity*, that is, can furnish conditions of the possibility of all knowledge of objects' (A89/B122).

3. 'The objective validity of the categories as a priori concepts rests . . . on the fact that, so far as the form of thought is concerned, through them alone does experience become possible. They relate of necessity and a priori to objects of experience, for the reason that only by means of them can any object whatsoever of experience be thought' (A93/B126).

4. 'If we can prove that by their [the categories'] means alone an object can be thought, this will be a sufficient deduction of them, and will justify their objective validity' (A96).

5. ' . . . the manifold in a given intuition is necessarily subject to the categories' (B143).

6. ' . . . the categories are conditions of the possibility of experience' (B161).

The difficulty with these formulations of the task of the Deduction is that they either (as in 1–4) make the Deduction seem redundant, or (5 and 6) make what seem to be quite impossible demands on it.

---

[1] Kemp Smith has ' . . . how these concepts can relate to objects which they yet do not obtain from any experience'. What Kant is saying here is, I think, clear enough, though his own words are certainly obscure: 'man aber doch wissen muss, wie diese Begriffe sich auf Objekte beziehen können, die sie doch aus keiner Erfahrung hernehmen.'

First, 1 above, the question of how the categories can relate a priori to objects, seems to be essentially the issue for Schematism, the question of how the categories can find application, can 'determine objects'. The role cast for the Deduction in 3 and 4, on the other hand, seems to have been already filled by the Clue, the derivation of the categories from the judgment forms. The very manner in which the categories were there introduced already guarantees that they apply necessarily to all possible objects of thought. Since the judgment forms 'yield an exhaustive inventory of the powers of the understanding', since they express functions without which no thought is possible—and since the categories are simply those same functions considered as having verticality, as applying to objects—it follows immediately that only by means of the categories can an object be thought. (See also A79/B105.) But this we are now told in 4 above 'will be a sufficient deduction of them and will justify their objective validity' (also 2). And from it we can trivially infer that 'only by means of them can any object whatsoever of experience be thought' (3).

Finally, the formulations of 5 and 6, if these are interpreted as going beyond 1–4, raise different problems. If they are taken as claiming that experience, or the manifold, is necessarily subject to the categories not merely, as in 3, in that it is thought, or thinkable, but somehow absolutely, then these claims become quite mysterious. For how, one must ask, could the categories, given what they are, mere functions of unity, possibly provide for anything *but* the thinkability, the intelligibility, of anything? We could hardly suppose that they could somehow actually bring into existence the manifold of intuition (or appearances, objects of experience). And, indeed, any such supposition would sharply conflict with what is quite fundamental Kantian doctrine: ' . . . appearances can certainly be given in intuition independently of functions of the understanding' (A90/B122); ' . . . intuition stands in no need whatsoever of the functions of thought' (A91/B123); 'our understanding can only *think* and for intuition must look to the senses' (B135). Any intuition *in so far as it can be thought* stands in need of such functions of course; but that, it appears, has been adequately established before we begin the Transcendental Deduction.

So what is the Deduction for? Our difficulty is this. Clearly the Deduction is supposed to show that some particular activity or undertaking requires the employment of the categories; yet it seems that the only kind of activity which could reasonably be thought to require the categories has already, in the Clue, been shown to do so. This difficulty is not created by but it is indeed underlined by many of the remarks Kant makes as to the purpose of the Deduction.

The main source of this difficulty is, I believe, an inveterate clumsiness in Kant's manner of presenting the issues. Too often he fails to tell us which statements he regards as already established (or for that matter as self-evident), and which statements he means to argue for later. The way out of the present difficulty is to see that that crucial claim made in the Clue—the claim to the effect that the judgment forms 'specify the understanding completely and yield an exhaustive inventory of its powers', is not in any way established in the Clue; it awaits argument at a later stage. Let us look once again at the Clue. The table of judgment forms, from which Kant derives the categories, is, it will be remembered, borrowed with few and minor alterations from formal logic: 'Here, then, the labours of the logicians are ready at hand . . .'.[2] Now, many, though importantly not all, of the things Kant says about these judgment forms can be taken as simply repeating what logical theory has maintained about them. Thus Kant is entitled to say, without having himself to argue, that the forms are 'logical functions in all possible judgments' (A79/B105), that they are 'moments of thought in judgments' (A73/B98), and that they 'give unity to the various representations in a judgment' (A79/B104). These are the sorts of things that (traditional) logic can reasonably be thought to teach; all possible judgments or propositions involve

[2] *Prolegomena to Any Future Metaphysics,* ed. Lewis White Beck (Indianapolis, 1950), §19.

these and these logical functions. In the making of any judgment the mind unifies the elements by these and these operations. But when Kant says of the forms that they 'specify the understanding completely, and yield an exhaustive inventory of its powers', he is, without giving notice, going much further. He is no longer listing and characterizing as such the roles in judgment of these forms; he is telling us that judgment (as defined by these forms) is necessarily at work whenever the human understanding operates at all. A person does not understand, or realize, or come to see, anything whatever unless he judges—where judgment is defined by the functions of unity. Formal logic is not in a position to make this sort of statement, nor is the statement at all self-evident. It clearly needs a quite separate argument.

What is true of the claim that the judgment forms 'specify the understanding completely . . .' is also true of another important remark, made early in the Clue, where Kant explicitly restricts the scope of the understanding to the capacity to form judgments: 'Now we can reduce all acts of the understanding to judgments, and the *understanding* may therefore be represented as *a faculty of judgment*' (A69/B94). From this remark it is an easy step to the claim that the judgment forms 'specify the understanding completely . . .'; if judging is all that the understanding can do, then the functions of judgment will tell us all there is to tell about that faculty's work. But, again, that judging is all the understanding can do is not obvious—just why it should not be taken as obvious we will go into more fully below—nor is it argued for in the Clue. Nor, incidentally, would it be right to take Kant to be here *legislating* this restriction, laying it down by decree that only cases of judging are to be counted as acts of the understanding. To do this would be to sweep any question about the nature of understanding under the rug and, as we shall see, would deprive Kant of the possibility of giving any reasoned support to his claim (against his predecessors) that intuition, confrontation with objects, is insufficient for understanding. The proposition that judging is all that the understanding can do, though blithely and innocently asserted, without so much as a comment as to its status, in the Clue, is a central Kantian doctrine; the argument for it is postponed until the Transcendental Deduction.

But we need to say more than this to convince ourselves fully that the Transcendental Deduction is a necessary part of Kant's account of the nature of the understanding. In particular, we need to see more clearly what is involved in the idea of 'understanding something', the idea of 'thought of objects', such that it is necessary to *argue* that all understanding (or thought) of objects involves the judgment forms and hence the categories. We must, that is, come to see just how it is that the thesis at issue is not an obvious or trivial thesis. How can it seem startling, or even significant, that there can be no understanding without judgment? What is the content of the claim that is being denied in the denial that there can be any thought of objects without the categories? We gave the beginning of an answer to this question a moment ago: what is being denied is that someone can understand or realize or come to see anything at all unless he judges, employs the categories of the understanding. We need to elaborate this theme.

The question at issue, the question for the Transcendental Deduction, can be put like this. Granted that we, adult speakers of the language, can and do articulate our understanding, our apprehension, of what is before us in judgmental or propositional form, is it also the case that there can *be* no understanding or apprehension which is not articulable in this way *by the person who has that understanding*? It might well seem not. For why should there not be such a thing as an *Urerkenntnis*, a primeval understanding or grasping of an item, where such a grasping consists simply in the presence of that item in consciousness? Why, in particular, should not the mere occurrence of data in a sentient creature be sufficient for the apprehending (if only, perhaps, on a rudimentary level) of those data? Why should *any* grasping of a thing in consciousness require that very special kind of unifying of data that is brought about by logical functions of judgment? Why, without those functions, should any presence of data leave us, visually sentient though we nevertheless be, *blind*? (And why 'blind', and not merely 'mute'? For indeed—let us concede—we could not without employing those forms *articulate* our understanding of anything.)

Kant's theory of the nature of the understanding must address these questions. If it does not address them it is not a theory of the understanding, of what it is to grasp something by the intellect, but simply an analysis of the machinery of judgment. To put the point another way, without the Transcendental Deduction, where these questions are addressed, and relying solely on the Clue and the Schematism, we would have no more than the view that in all judgments about objects we *portray* those objects as totalities, realities, substances, causes, etc.; that is, we would know only that all (including empirical) judgments involve the (schematized) categories. But this, understood in the carefully qualified way in which it must be understood here, is a thesis with which even a Berkeley or a Hume might have been brought to agree. For it says no more than that every fully articulated empirical judgment, every thought about experienced objects that finds expression in a declarative sentence, involves the categories. It does *not* say, nor does it imply, that there can be no apprehension whatever of anything empirical without the categories (see e.g. B122/A90). It does not preclude the possibility of forming ideas from impressions alone, of simply recording in consciousness, without the aid of any such logical functions, whatever is presented to the senses. A dyed-in-the-wool empiricist might allow that the proposition 'This dog is black', unlike the word-list 'the-is-dog-black', involves such functions, obeys such rules. And I see no reason why he should not also allow that the simple utterance, or thought-content, 'black', so long as it is regarded by the utterer or thinker as mere shorthand for the fully fledged proposition, obeys those same rules. To allow this would be to allow no more than that our language is rule-governed, that the vehicle for expressing our thought follows certain (perhaps arbitrary) conventions. In allowing this the empiricist would not—and rightly so—consider himself to be conceding to Kant the view that only in so far as one employs these rules is it true *that one really sees the dog to have that colour* (that it is black). For, he will argue, though one who has mastered that language might well, in thinking 'black' in these circumstances, be simply abbreviating for himself a thought of the form 'This dog is black', one who had no language, an infant, say, or an animal, could surely none the less apprehend the colour of the dog simply in unarticulatedly attending to, visually focusing upon, what is before him. And further, the fact that we, in reporting his experience, might *impute* judgment to him ('he sees that p') does not mean that he, the infant or animal, must therefore after all be employing the logical functions of judgment; *ex hypothesi* he cannot do this. What it does mean, the empiricist will claim, is that the understanding, the apprehension, the thought that we *record* by means of these functions can exist independently of them.

In this way, I suggest, an empiricist might accept what is established in the Clue and the Schematism, and still, consistently with his empiricism, argue that sensible intuition is sufficient for understanding, apprehending what is given in experience. Whatever it is in Kant that argues against this claim must play an integral role in his theory of the nature of understanding.

I have dwelt on this theme at some length both in order to indicate the need in Kant's theory for a transcendental deduction of the categories, and also to give a fuller picture of the scope and ramifications of the thesis that the Deduction is meant to demonstrate. We have now touched upon a number of versions and implications of this thesis: that the logical functions of judgment specify the understanding completely; that all acts of the understanding are judgments; that the categories are necessary for all thought (not merely for all judgment) of objects; that judgment, and therefore the employment of the categories, is necessary for experience of anything; that intuitions without concepts are blind. I have tried to

indicate how these various statements are intercon-
nected. Understanding anything requires judgment, and
therefore the categories; it is that without which we
cannot apprehend, are blind to, what is given in intuition. All this is, of course, still quite skeletal. We are not
yet in a position, without considering the actual argument of the Deduction, to see why these connections are
supposed to hold; we do not yet know how it is that
employing the functions of unity with regard to objects
of intuition can make it possible for us to 'see', apprehend, those objects, where we would otherwise be 'blind'
to them. This means also that we cannot yet remedy a
certain vagueness and obscurity about that central
notion that I have variously been calling 'understanding',
'realizing', 'grasping', 'apprehending', 'seeing' something.
Until we come to see the reasons Kant gives, in the
Deduction, for saying that this 'act' requires the logical
functions of judgment, we are not in a position to be at all
precise about what it amounts to.[3]

Before we come, in Chapter 5, to the Deduction itself
we must briefly consider yet a further, and most
important, version of the thesis that it, the Deduction, is
meant to demonstrate, another question that the Deduction is designed to answer. This is the question, as Kant
puts it, of 'how *subjective conditions of thought* can
have *objective validity*' (A89/B122). This, in various
subforms, is perhaps the most prominent formulation in

---

[3] A note about Kant's terminology. Kant's preferred term for the act which I
have been calling by these various names is '*erkennen*' and for its product,
'*eine Erkenntnis*'. Norman Kemp Smith's translation of these as, respectively,
'know' and 'knowledge' (and, obscurely, as 'modes of knowledge' in the plural)
is in most contexts mistaken. '*Erkenntnis*' as used by Kant, is typically a count
noun with a standard plural, and *Erkenntnisse* can as easily be false as true
(e.g. A58/B83). Max-Müller's (and Meiklejohn's) 'cognize' and 'cognition' are
preferable in these respects. *Erkennen*, in Kant, always has an (intentional)
object, i.e. a thing or state of affairs that the mind represents to itself in having
something presented to it. This will be our subject in Chapter 5. *Denken*
(thinking), by contrast, does not always have an intentional object, e.g. in
moral matters; and *Sinnlichkeit* (sensibility) cannot have one. The thesis of
Kant's that is to be examined in the following chapters is that experience
(*Erfahrung*), which is nothing other than empirical *Erkenntnis* (B166), and
which is the only grasping of objects of which human beings are capable, is
possible only through the employment of the schematized categories.

the *Critique* of the task of the Deduction. It is the one
with which Kant first raises the entire issue (the *'quid
juris'* question, A84/B116 ff.), and it is the one for reason
of which he calls the argument a 'deduction' (i.e. a
justification) of the categories. We must inquire into how
this version stands in relation to the others we have
considered. In particular, what has the question of the
objective validity of the categories got to do with the
question of their necessity for apprehending or grasping
whatever is given in intuition? How can a single
argument answer both of these questions at once?

What would it mean for the categories to be merely
subjective conditions of thought, to *lack* objective validity? It would be for them to do no more than characterize
how we happen to be constructed to form thoughts about
things. A detailed look at the structure of human
language (as in the Clue) reveals that human beings are
such that they portray, think of, things presented to them
as totalities, substances, causes, etc. But this, for all we
know at this point, is nothing but a subjective fact about
people, a sort of quirk which has no implications
whatever for the nature of the things that our so carefully
constructed thought-structures represent. It may be the
case, for example, as far as the Clue and the Schematism
go, that the things we are aware of in our experience are
discrete and transitory items, all on a logical par, as it
were, and having no relations to one another apart from
contingent, empirical ones; and it may further be the
case that we are in fact aware of those items *as* being thus
discrete, transitory, only empirically related—yet we are
so constructed that when we put together thoughts about
those items, when we *discourse*, to others or to ourselves, about them, we are constrained to represent them
as having these or those non-empirical relations to one
another, of one inhering in another, of one as the effect of
another, etc. This hypothesis drives a wedge between
how things actually are, how we basically understand
them to be, in our direct awareness (intuition) of them,
on the one hand, and how we represent them in our
articulated, communicable thought-formations on the

other. To show that this hypothesis does not present us with a real possibility would be to show that there can be no awareness of things at all which does not represent those things in that articulated way; and this is the thesis we have been speaking of all along.[4] The question of the objective validity of the categories is thus the same question as that of their necessity for understanding, grasping, apprehending anything.

And with this we also have the solution to the puzzle about the first of the five formulations of the task of the Deduction that we quoted earlier in this chapter. That formulation was as follows: '. . .we are faced by the problem how these concepts [the categories] can relate to objects when they are nevertheless not derived from any experience of objects. The explanation of the manner in which concepts can thus relate a priori to objects I entitle their transcendental deduction' (A85/B117). Our puzzle here was that this question, of how the categories can relate a priori to objects, seems to be just the question which the Schematism was designed to answer. But now we can, I think, note a difference. The question addressed by Schematism is this: How can the (unschematized) categories 'determine' objects, how can they describe, characterize, things in space and time, when they are, after all, nothing but functions of unity baldly conceived as applying to things? And we give the answer by providing the categories with criteria for their application; once equipped with these criteria (schemata), they are fully fledged concepts. But providing criteria does not

[4] If Kant's argument is successful here then he will have answered a certain kind of sceptic, viz. a Humean one, one who questions whether, or denies that, the objects of our awareness actually contain the features that our talk (e.g. in causal and substantival terms) imputes to them. Kant will not be addressing the sort of sceptic, a transcendental realist, who questions whether things quite apart from the possibility of our being aware of them contain such features. So Kant is doubly misrepresented by those who take a 'transcendental argument' to be one which purports to show that our conceptual scheme depends on there actually being such things as this or that (e.g. material objects, other minds). For (a) the antecedent of that conditional posits, at best, subjective necessity; and (b) the consequent makes no reference to our awareness of things. See, e.g. Barry Stroud, 'Transcendental Arguments', *Journal of Philosophy*, lxv. 1968.

do everything that needs to be done. Of the categories, even when schematized, we can still ask: How can these concepts really be objective, how can they really be concepts of objects, of objects we meet with in experience, when, after all, they are in no way derived from experience of those objects? The existence of application criteria does not settle this question. The fact that we have a criterion for the application of the concept *cause and effect* (or for that matter of the concept *fate*, or *witch*) does not mean that there is therefore no longer any question of how that concept can relate to objects. So long as what it means for *a* to cause *b* 'goes beyond', as it does, what we count as the criterion for its application (the schema, regular succession) there will still be the question of whether one thing in our awareness really ever does cause anything else, or whether, instead, that is just a fact about how we think about things. This is, of course, again the question of the objective validity of the categories. The question is dramatized in this way: the very fact that categories owe nothing to experience, that they are *pure* concepts, might seem to be their undoing as far as their claim to be concepts of objects of experience is concerned. There is a clear and urgent need to show how it is that they are not mere subjective impositions.

5

Sentience, Apperception, and Language

We have now arrived at a broad if still somewhat unrefined idea of what the Transcendental Deduction will try to demonstrate. We anticipate that Kant will attempt to prove that there can be no awareness, no apprehending or understanding, no grasping of data in consciousness, which does not involve judgment and therefore the categories; there is no such thing as an *Urerkenntnis*, an unmediated consciousness of something, which consists in nothing more than the occurrence of sensory data in a sentient being. In short, an argument is to be produced which shows that, somehow, consciousness itself involves the categories.

Now it might well seem, once again, that any such argument is doomed from the start. For, on the one hand, is it not clear that a person, or, for that matter, any sentient creature, is conscious or aware of something simply in so far as he or it (or his or its mind— *Gemüt* A19/B33) is 'affected'? And it is, as we have seen, both implausible and contrary to Kant's central teaching, to suggest that categories of the understanding are at work just in so far as a creature is sensibly affected. But if, on the other hand, Kant means by 'consciousness' something over and above the capacity to be sensorily affected, if 'consciousness' is redefined to include some additional factor—for example the capacity to conceive or portray things as having this or that particular status— then indeed it might become plausible to suggest that the categories are involved in all consciousness, but at the cost of losing all critical relevance to the views that Kant

means to refute. We do not begin to undermine Hume's
doctrine that impressions are sufficient for the having of
ideas by stipulating in advance that we will count as
ideas only items of certain logical sorts, items that
conform to these or those specific patterns.

If Kant's argument is to stand any chance of being
successful, he must not in any way legislate that
sensibility is insufficient for consciousness, nor may he
introduce any new and enlarged conception of consciousness, any conception which is not fully shared by his
predecessors. What he must do is argue that consciousness, as we must all understand it—Hume too—necessarily involves the categories. There might seem to be an
obvious objection to this. Doesn't, or wouldn't, Hume
equate consciousness (at least on its most basic level)
with sensibility? Wouldn't he simply *mean* by 'consciousness', at that level, the having of representations,
the capacity to be affected? The answer is No; no-one
means this by 'consciousness'! To see how this is so, we
must turn now to the actual argument of the Deduction.

Kant says at B131–2:

It must be possible for the 'I think' to accompany all my
representations; for otherwise something would be represented
in me which could not be thought at all, and that is equivalent
to saying that the representation would either[1] be impossible,
or at least would be nothing to me.

This claim serves as a premiss for the main argument of
the Transcendental Deduction of the Categories: pure
apperception, the necessity of being able to ascribe
representations, or data of consciousness, to oneself
requires, Kant will argue, that those representations be
unified in one consciousness; and such unification is
achievable only by means of judgment, and so necessitates the employment of the categories.[2]

---

[1] I am restoring Kant's 'entweder' here, omitted by Kemp Smith. The
omission makes the important last phrase of the sentence look like an
afterthought. See below.
[2] This, in a nutshell, is the main argument of the Deduction as I am
understanding it. It is best represented in the B edition (B131–43). The
argument is less clearly visible, at least as a separate strand, in the A edition.

Keeping in mind its prospective role as a premiss, what are we to make of this claim? It does not seem hard to get an intuitive grasp on the idea of self-ascribability as such. It is some sort of capacity for self-consciousness, the ability not merely to suffer a representation, but to reflect on, or note, the fact that one is having it, the ability not merely to have the datum red inflicted upon one, but to see oneself as seeing red. It is the difference between the hearing of a noise and the thought: 'I hear something'. That we have such a capacity in general is, I suppose, beyond question. But Kant's claim is not just that this capacity for self-consciousness exists, but that it is necessary. The question we need to ask is: Why? What is the capacity for self-consciousness necessary *for*? On pain of what, according to Kant, must every representation be capable of being accompanied by the 'I think'? It is perhaps tempting, given B131–2, to answer this question in the following way. The capacity for self-consciousness is necessary with regard to any representation I might have, for otherwise that representation would simply not exist, it would not *be* anything in the mind. For there to exist such a thing as a representation, an impingement on consciousness, is for the person who has it to be capable of ascribing it to himself; consciousness, the very having of representations, presupposes the capacity for self-consciousness. That this is Kant's view of the matter is, I think, quite widely held. I shall argue, however, that it crucially distorts his position, so much so as to completely block from our view the central point of the Transcendental Deduction. To see more clearly what the view in question contains I shall make use of an article, by Paul Guyer,[3] which attributes the view

---

[3] Paul Guyer, 'Kant on Apperception and a priori Synthesis', *American Philosophical Quarterly*, July, 1980. See also Guyer's more recent *Kant and the Claims of Knowledge* (Cambridge, 1987), esp. Pt. II, where similar arguments occur. (Another recent criticism on parallel lines is by T. E. Wilkerson, 'Kant on Self-Consciousness', *Philosophical Quarterly*, January, 1980.) Guyer does not find fault with the later stages of the argument of the Deduction; indeed he regards the thesis that any representation I can ascribe to myself is subject to the categories (or at least 'to a certain kind of synthesis', ('Kant on Apperception', p. 208)) as 'analytic'. But he rightly sees that Kant

to Kant, and takes him to task for it. Guyer interprets Kant as claiming that 'I cannot have a representation which I cannot recognize as my own' (p. 209). And that claim, he says, is quite unsupported by Kant: 'Kant has no argument at all for the thesis that all consciousness is self-consciousness, but only a conflation of the two concepts' (p. 210). He (Kant) proceeds in no way to prove, but 'just to assume that consciousness is self-consciousness, or that I must be capable of self-ascription whenever I am capable of consciousness at all' (ibid.). As to the question of why Kant should make such an assumption, or conflate these two different concepts, Guyer suggests the following:

Perhaps Kant's error stems from tacitly thinking of consciousness only from a first-person point of view . . . It does seem indisputable that whichever of one's own states one can recognize as states of consciousness must also involve self-consciousness, for to recognize one's state as conscious (or anything else, for that matter) first requires recognizing it as one's own state. But from this it does not follow that one could not have a state of consciousness without being able to ascribe it to oneself, or without self-consciousness, for there might be cases in which one is conscious without recognizing it . . . For example: if we regard dreams as modifications of consciousness, but also regard the occurrence of rapid eye movements (REMs) as good empirical evidence for the simultaneous occurrence of dreaming, then we may regard our own observation of REMs in another as evidence that the other is conscious at a given moment, even though it later turns out that the other person himself has no memory of his dream, and thus cannot ascribe consciousness to himself with respect to the moment in question—or accompany what we know to have been his consciousness with self-consciousness.[4]

One could cite many similar instances, similar in that they are cases of consciousness without self-consciousness. We have every reason to believe that an animal or a

means to argue for a stronger, and 'synthetic' thesis (ibid.), viz. that consciousness itself is impossible without that same synthesis afforded by the categories.

[4] Guyer, 'Kant on Apperception', pp. 210–11.

newborn infant has states of consciousness (e.g. hunger, pain), and at the same time, in many cases, every reason to deny it any conception of itself as a subject of states, and so any capacity for the self-ascription of those states. But the situation is worse even than this. For if Kant does hold the thesis which Guyer attributes to him, namely that there can be no representation, or state of consciousness, without self-consciousness, then, given the rest of the Transcendental Deduction, it seems he will be committed to the view that every sentient creature, every house-fly and inchworm, is equipped with a human understanding and synthesizes its data by means of categories. And it will be no use protesting at this point that Kant's inquiry is directed from the beginning only to human beings and not to sentient beings generally, that we are concerned only with the implications of *people's* representations, *human* states of consciousness. For it would be neither Kantian nor desirable to distinguish human beings from other sentient creatures at the level of representations as such. There is no reason to suppose that the pain of pulled hair is in itself something different in kind in a cat than in a person (particularly so when we remember, with Guyer, the third-person, behavioural, grounds for ascribing such representations). If wincing and jerking the head are sufficient grounds for ascribing pain, in these circumstances, then there is no relevant distinction to be drawn between the cat's state of consciousness and the person's. If there is a difference it is not in the representation itself, but in what the human understanding, in the one case, can do with it. But if the very existence of any representation is conditional on what the understanding can do with it (the thesis Guyer attributes to Kant), then the cat, and presumably the house-fly, as well as the human being must apply the categories.

Guyer remarks on the fact that the thesis that all consciousness is self-consciousness is unsupported by Kant, and that it is implausible (REMs, etc.). What he does not point out is the depth of the conflict between that thesis and so much, apparently, of the rest of Kant's teaching. It is not only that the thesis is inconsistent with remarks which state or imply that non-human animals have a sensibility but no self-consciousness, no categories,[5] but also that it conflicts with what seems to be the very basis of the distinction between sensibility and understanding. Sensibility, 'the capacity for receiving representations' (A50/B74) is, we are repeatedly told, utterly distinct from understanding, 'the power of grasping an object [*einen Gegenstand zu erkennen*] through these representations' (ibid.). The former yields intuitions, the latter concepts. 'Without sensibility no object would be given to us, without understanding no object would be thought. Thoughts without content are empty, intuitions without concepts are blind. It is therefore just as necessary to make our concepts sensible, that is, to add the object to them in intuition, as to make our intuitions intelligible, that is, to bring them under concepts' (A51/B75). It seems to me that the force of these remarks cannot be explained away by allusions to the picturesqueness of faculty terminology. The point of what Kant is saying here is quite lost if he in fact holds that the very existence of sensorily received representations requires apperception and the categories. Our capacity for receiving representations is something, Kant is saying here, that is by itself *insufficient* for knowledge of objects. This would be grossly misleading, if not simply false, if the only kind of representation there can possibly be is one which is self-ascribable, which is consequently synthesized with others by means of the categories, and which therefore affords knowledge of objects. Moreover, Kant is making some *special* point,

---

[5] See e.g. the 1789 letter to Marcus Herz: Without the categories, Kant claims, 'I would not even be able to know that I have sense-data; consequently for me, as a knowing being, they would be absolutely nothing. They would still (I imagine myself to be an animal) carry on their play in an orderly fashion, as representations connected according to empirical laws of association, and thus even have an influence on my feeling and desire, without my being aware of them . . . ' (Arnulf Zweig, *Kant's Philosophical Correspondence* (Chicago, 1967), 153–4). Cf. also *Anthropology from a Pragmatic Point of View*, in *Kant's Gesammelte Schriften*, vol. 7 (Berlin, 1917), 127, and *Preisschrift über die Fortschritte der Metaphysik*, *Schriften*, 20, 270.

surely, in saying that intuitions without concepts are *blind*, that they need to be brought under concepts to be made *intelligible*. Whatever this special point (or points) might be, it is altogether nullified by the thesis that intuitions without concepts simply do not exist. Finally, there are remarks which go directly against the thesis in question: '. . . appearances can certainly be given in intuition independently of functions of the understanding' (A90/B122); 'intuition stands in no need whatsoever of functions of thought' (A91/B123); it 'can be given prior to all thought' (B132).

None of this by itself, of course, refutes Guyer's interpretation of Kant's position. It may be that the major thesis of the Transcendental Deduction is implausible and unsupported, and radically inconsistent with much else in Kant's philosophy. But I do not believe that it is. I shall argue for a different interpretation. I believe that Kant's thesis here, far from conflicting with the doctrine of the separation of faculties, in fact deepens our understanding of it, and, for the first time, provides it with real justification. And it is a considerably subtler and more powerful thesis than the one we have been considering.

Let us turn once more to that 'premiss' in the B Deduction where the notion of self-consciousness is introduced: 'It must be possible for the "I think" to accompany all my representations; for otherwise something would be represented in me which could not be thought at all, and that is equivalent to saying that the representation would either be impossible, or at least would be nothing to me' (B131–2).

This would be a strangely circuitous way of putting things if what Kant really wanted to say was simply that '*whatever* is to count as a representation at all must be fit for self-ascription',[6] that 'I cannot have a representation which I cannot recognize as my own'.[7] That the representation 'would be impossible' is not put forward as a

[6] Guyer, 'Kant on Apperception', p. 209.
[7] Ibid.

simple and immediate consequence of my incapacity to
ascribe it to myself. The remark that it would be
impossible is a gloss on another remark, and only a part
of that gloss, and is itself disjoined with, and qualified by,
yet a further remark. Let us look at the entire sentence
more carefully. What is put forward as the first consequence, before the gloss, of my being unable to ascribe
a representation to myself is that 'otherwise something
would be represented in me which could not be thought
at all'. This is not at all the same as saying: otherwise the
representation could not be had, received, felt, could not
exist. The reference to *thought* is crucial. What Kant is
saying is, I believe, this. If I could not ascribe a given
representation to myself, that representation could not
serve as the means, the material, for my thinking, or
forming a concept of, anything at all. Now there is indeed
a sense in which a representation by means of which
nothing can be thought or conceived (i.e. which has no
intentional object) is not a representation at all, for it
precisely fails to represent (*vorstellen*) anything to me.
For something to be 'represented in me which could not
be thought at all' *is* in a way contradictory. *That* is why
the representation would be 'impossible'. It would not
say anything, wouldn't be anything or mean anything to
me, would not represent anything. Part of what encourages a position like Guyer's is that Kant is here insisting
on the strict connotations of his term '*Vorstellung*'; as if
to say: 'a *Vorstellung* that does not represent anything is
not a *Vorstellung*.' But of course *Vorstellung* was not
introduced, in the *Critique*, as an item that represents (or
presents, ideates, points to) something. It is not as if the
thing which is called a *Vorstellung* depends for its
existence on its having some intentional object. Sensibility is itself defined in terms of the reception of representations; to be sensorily affected at all is to have them
(A19/B33). So why did Kant choose this heavily loaded
and question-begging term? Why not something more
neutral in this respect, like 'mental content', 'state of
mind', 'state of consciousness' (Guyer's favoured term)?
At least part of the answer is that human experience is

such that when someone is sensorily affected, say visually, his being so normally or paradigmatically constitutes there being represented in him (presented to him, the idea formed in him of) an object of a certain sort, for example something red. (This does not mean that the affection is *produced* by something red—though that will also be paradigmatically true.) Kant's whole interest, of course, is on the conditions that are necessary for a sensation to constitute such a (re)presenting.

But none of this implies that in the absence of there being something represented to me, in the absence of there being an (intentional) object of my thought, nothing would have occurred in me after all, that my sensibility could not have been affected. What Kant is saying is that an affection, a state of sensibility, a visual sensation, say, does not provide an object for thought, does not yield an idea of anything (e.g. the idea *red*) unless I can ascribe it to myself. The capacity of self-consciousness is put forward, then, not as a condition of the reception of representations, of the very functioning of sensibility, but as a condition under which alone those representations, the data of sensibility, can represent anything to us, that is, can give us so much as a thought or an idea of anything.

Now we do not yet know *why* Kant thinks, or why anyone should think, that the capacity for self-consciousness—and therefore, anticipating, synthesis by means of the categories—is necessary for consciousness of anything. It may be that the thesis remains as implausible and as unsupported as Guyer holds it to be. But we do now have some idea, I hope, of what it is that apperception and the categories are necessary for. And we can begin to see in some detail why it is that Kant is dissatisfied with an empiricist picture of consciousness, with the view that sensibility is sufficient for there being objects before the mind. The point is not the implausible one, which Guyer imputes to Kant, that sensibility itself rests on something else (apperception and the categories) —nor is it, incidentally, that Kant wishes to include in the very notion of there being objects before the mind some element (objectivity, independence) which his empiricist predecessors had not dreamed of including. Kant's point is that that essential feature of the data of sensibility, the feature so insisted upon by Locke and Hume, namely their capacity to be captured in thought, to be 'originals' for the mind, their reproducibility or copyability in and by the understanding—that feature is not provided for by their *being* data of sensibility, but is subject to the special conditions of self-ascribability and hence the categories.

Locke and Hume held that our being sensorily affected is sufficient for our having ideas. It is tempting perhaps to see this doctrine as one which *reduces* ideas to affections (or copies thereof), one which *defines* understanding in terms solely of sensibility. But this is quite wrong. Locke's belief that our simplest ideas amount to nothing but sensory data is a substantive one connecting understanding with sensibility, it is not merely the belief that there are simple sensory data. And when Hume announced that our simple ideas are nothing but copies of impressions, he was not saying that the fainter items are copies of the stronger ones—let's call them 'ideas'. Ideas are concepts, not data. To have an idea, for Locke or Hume (or anyone else) does not *mean* to be (actually or in facsimile) sensorily affected; it means to perceive something, to grasp something in thought, to have something before the mind. The empiricists' doctrine is after all not a doctrine of sensibility, but one of understanding, to wit, the doctrine that the fundamental building blocks of understanding are to be found in sensibility alone. It is the doctrine, to put it another way, that for something to be true *for* one it is sufficient that something be sensorily true *of* one. This is the view that Kant is denying; he is claiming that without apperception and the categories the data of sensibility remain mere data and cannot reach the understanding; without the categories nothing can be true for one. (We will see later in this chapter that the claim that to be conscious of anything is for something to be true for one does not (as it might seem to) beg a question against the empiricists.)

Perhaps none of this is as yet very clear or very convincing. In particular, the whole notion of understanding, having an idea, grasping in thought, etc., is still frustratingly hazy; and one might well suspect that Kant is (or that we are) overplaying this notion, and, correspondingly, underplaying the notion of the data of sensibility. For, it will be argued, sensibility is, after all, even for Kant, a compartment of the *mind*. It is not, for instance, a merely physiological capacity, the possession and functioning of organs and nerves, or whatever. And the mind, for all of these philosophers, descendants of Descartes, is the arena of consciousness. To be sensorily affected is therefore already to be in a conscious state. And to be in a conscious state *is* for there to be something before the mind, it is to have ideas, to grasp something in consciousness. And so it will seem once again that either Kant must, implausibly, deny that sentience is possible without apperception and the categories, or he must, in a question-begging way, redefine the notion of having something before the mind, and so allow Hume and others to escape his clutches.

How can Kant deny that to be sensorily affected is to be conscious? Is he in fact denying this? We must not allow the word 'conscious' to play tricks on us here. There is no good reason why Kant should object to the suggestion that to be sensorily affected is to be in a conscious state. It is not as if we are, in the absence of apperception, somehow anaesthetized. To be in a sensory state, in that state, for example, that typically results from a blow to the head or an empty stomach, is, as such, to suffer, and to suffer is to be conscious. There is nothing that Kant need find wrong with this sort of talk; pain, hunger, sensations and representations generally, are, as such, states, or modifications of, or impingements on, consciousness.[8] The mistake, Kant would say, is at the next stage; that is, in the belief that to be in a conscious state is as such to *grasp something* in consciousness, that it is for there to be something before the mind. It is Kant's

[8] Guyer, 'Kant on Apperception', p. 209.

claim that states of consciousness do not entail objects of consciousness; to be hungry is not *per se* to grasp something, to be dazzled is not yet to perceive something; to be in pain is not, in itself, for something to be true for one. Even if it were the case, which I suspect it is not, that whenever any creature is sensorily affected (and thus in a conscious state) it grasped or held something in thought, it would still not be the case that its doing so could be explicated or accounted for by sole reference to the manner in which it was sensorily affected. We are not given an understanding of what it is for someone to perceive, or conceive, what is before his eyes to be red (or to be anything) by being told in detail how he is visually affected. No description in terms solely of his sensory states can make manifest what is meant by saying that he has the *thought*: 'This is red (or whatever)', that (its being) red is the (intentional) *object of his mind*, not merely the *content of his state*. (Of course this distinction collapses if its being the content of one's state entails that one thinks it is! We need something other than a first-person criterion for states of sensibility. We will comment on this in a moment.)

The point we have been making here might be misunderstood. It might look as if we have been claiming that all perceiving is thinking, and therefore 'propositional'. That to see something red (or F) is always to take it to be red (or F). And that is surely false. But it is not the point we are making. Our claim is, rather, that *if* something visually (or otherwise) present is to be capable of being material for the understanding—if it is such that one can record it, reflect upon it, report it, generalize from it, deliberate about it, etc., *then* one must have taken it to be something, for example red. Where it is true that someone sees something F without taking it to be F, 'see' cannot there be first-personal, it is exclusively third-personal. We will consider later in this chapter the relation of the idea of first-person 'access' (it isn't *access* at all) to that of (intentional) objects of consciousness.

But are states (or contents) of consciousness and objects of consciousness really distinct items? It is absolutely crucial to Kant's enterprise that they are and can be shown to be. If they cannot ultimately be distinguished, it cannot be shown that the categories, while not themselves a part of sensibility, are nevertheless required for, and so valid of, all objects of consciousness.

Why does the distinction between objects of consciousness and sensory states seem so precarious? It is not as if the *expressions* for these sound as if they mean the same. Yet the view that for red to be the content of one's sensory state is already for it to be the object of one's mind, for it to be what one is conscious of, is an extremely attractive view. One wants to say: 'If I am in a conscious state, then there is to that extent something of which I am conscious.' And what is that? Well, at the very least, the state itself; if I am hungry, then hunger is what I am aware of in myself, I am conscious of being hungry; if red is the content of my state, then that fact (that it is the content of my state) is what I am aware of. Now the claim that any state *which I am conscious of having* presents me with an object of consciousness is not a claim that Kant would want to dispute. If I am aware of being hungry, then indeed there is an object of my consciousness—I am having the thought: 'I am hungry'. But what encourages the idea that *being hungry* itself is, or involves, that thought? At least part of the answer to that question is, I think, this. When in a philosophical frame of mind we consider what it is to be hungry, or, in general, what it is to be in this or that state, we look at the situation from a first-person point of view: 'Well, when *I'm* hungry, I am aware of . . .' That is to say, we do not consider hunger, the state of sensibility, simply as such; instead, we take a case where, as we want to say, we are aware of being in that state, where we already have the *thought* 'I am hungry', and *then* ask what it is of which we are there aware. And the answer: 'I am aware of my hunger, aware that I'm hungry', is then, to be sure, readily forthcoming. But these manœuvres do not establish the intended direct connection between sensibility and understanding, between an affection and a thought, a state of consciousness and an object of consciousness. These manœuvres take place only along paths which are already well within the confines of the understanding, paths between thoughts and objects of consciousness.

From the first-person stance the distinction between something's being recognizably true *of* one and something's being true *for* one breaks down; for *if I can see* that it is true *of* me that S, then that I am, or have, S will be true *for me*. So we need, and Kant is committed to there being, something other than a first-person criterion for states of sensibility. If Kant is to uphold his thesis that sensibility does not presuppose understanding, he needs to allow that first-person recognition (e.g. 'I'm hungry') is not itself a constitutive part of what it is to be in a sensory state. Unfortunately, he does not seem to have noticed this, at least not clearly or consistently, and so he is led to making remarks (which ought to have puzzled him) which threaten the distinction he is otherwise at such pains to emphasize. Thus, for example, the two comments which Guyer cites in support of his interpretation:

All representations have a necessary relation to a *possible* empirical consciousness. For if they did not have this, and if it were altogether impossible to become conscious of them, this would practically amount to the admission of their non-existence (A117 n.).

. . .(Save through its relation to a consciousness that is at least possible, appearance could never be for us an object of knowledge, and so would be nothing to us; and since it has in itself no objective reality, but exists only in being known, it would be nothing at all.) (A120)

This last remark (A120) unlike both that from A117 n. and the 'I think' passage from B131–2, seems, when taken out of its context, to be a plain and unqualified statement of the position Guyer attributes to Kant. It is, however, preceded by two sentences, not cited by Guyer, which virtually contradict it: 'What is first given to us is appearance. When combined with consciousness, it is called perception. (Save through . . .)' This indicates that we *can* isolate appearance, and hence representations, from consciousness. See also A320/B376, where Kant classifies: 'The genus is representation in general (*repraesentatio*). Subordinate to it stands representation with consciousness (*perceptio*).' This clearly is Kant's basic position, and the one to which the doctrine of the separation of faculties commits him. Equally clearly, he has not come to terms with the question of what it is for there to be representations without consciousness of anything.

So, taking a first-person viewpoint on a state of consciousness converts that state into the thought that one has it. The mistake that results from taking this viewpoint exclusively is that one is thereby led, as Descartes was led, to suppose that first-person reflection is essential to the very existence of that state; as if a creature could not *be* hungry or in pain unless it recognized itself as so being, unless it had the thought: 'I am hungry (in pain).' To suppose this is to conceive the suffering of pain or hunger to lie not really in the pangs, but in the thought that one has them; as if, somehow, the pangs could not be felt, could not really hurt, unless they were made *objects* of consciousness. This is the mistake of supposing that all consciousness is intentional or representational, the mistake of denying that there really is such a thing as *sentience* at all.[9]

Now, the examples of states of consciousness that we have been employing here, namely hunger and pain, though they do serve to illustrate the points at issue, would probably not have been approved by Kant. For Kant seems to have believed, at least sometimes, not only that 'subjective' states are not *per se* objects of consciousness, but also that they cannot by any operation of the understanding become such *while still retaining their status as subjective states*. The operation

---

[9] This is not to deny that an adult speaker of the language is in fact capable of such reflection. It may even be the case that a *person* is, as Strawson has it, a being who is capable of self-ascribing, not on the basis of observation, what others ascribe to him on that basis (*Individuals* (London, 1959), ch. 3). My point is that this possibility of self-ascription is not implicit in concepts like *hunger* or *pain*, in what it means to be in such states.

that transforms an affection into an object of consciousness annihilates it in its status as an affection. Red, for
example, while 'initially' a subjective affection, a visual
sensation, in becoming an object of consciousness loses
its subjective character and becomes something objective, something visually perceived (NB The perception
need not be veridical; objective doesn't mean real—we're
talking of the intentional object still). What I am
conscious *of*, in being conscious of red, is no longer an
affection in me, but, for example the (alleged) colour of
this pen. But items like hunger and pain are not
susceptible to this transmutation. They are subjective
affections, states of the subject, from first to last.
Through them, unlike the case of red, nothing (no thing,
or property, or relation of things) is represented[10] (see e.g.
Critique of Judgment, B3, 4/A3, 4). For this reason they
cannot be, or yield, objects of awareness. Now, there may
be something right at the root of this idea; other
philosophers (Ryle, Wittgenstein) have argued that to feel
a pain is not to be aware of an object: I do not *judge* that I
am in pain. But it would be wrong to infer from this, as
Kant seems sometimes to do, that therefore subjective
states cannot in any way be objects for us—which means
that there can be no concepts of them, that they are not
subject to the categories at all.

So Kant would have disapproved of our use of the
examples of hunger and pain in this sense. We claimed
that what inclines one to suppose that merely to be in a
state of consciousness is already to have an object for
one's consciousness is that in reflecting on such matters
one tends to take a first-person standpoint on one's
conscious states. And taking this standpoint converts
what is mere affection into the thought that one is so
affected—it transforms one's hunger into the thought
that one is hungry and so makes of it an object of one's
consciousness. But if Kant believes, as we have now

---

[10] We may of course choose to view hunger (unlike pain) not merely as a
state of sensibility (induced by lack of food) but as a desire-for-food, and thus as
representational. What I am denying is only that it is, *qua* state of sensibility,
representational.

suggested, that there can be no such thought, no thought that one is affected in this or that way, then he could hardly accept our account (using such examples as hunger or pain) of how it is that one supposes that affections are, as such, objects of consciousness. At best, he could perhaps allow that we are subject to the illusion that hunger or pain can be objects of our awareness, that we can have the thought: 'I am hungry (in pain)'. (But then it is quite unclear how the possibility of such an illusion could be explained by Kant. How can one so much as seem to have the thought: 'I am hungry', when no such thought is possible at all?).

In any case, whether or not Kant would approve of our use of hunger and pain to exemplify and support his thesis, it is clearly important that we be able to generalize from such affections. For Kant's thesis is quite unrestricted: in no case does the reception of data *per se* amount to there being something before the mind. The point must hold in the case of visual or tactile or auditory data quite as much as it holds in the case of pain or hunger. It must be as true when the content of our sensibility is a colour or a movement or a noise. There is a special difficulty standing in the way of seeing this clearly—which is the chief reason why we used pain and hunger as our initial examples. It is particularly difficult, perhaps impossible, to subtract from colours, movements, etc., their intentionality or representationality, their status as objects of consciousness. Colours and movements, it might be said, just *are* things perceived, things *for us*; if you subtract that from them you are left with nothing. This may well be so. But it would be wrong to take that fact as demonstrating that simply to be chromatically affected, or to be visually responsive to movement, is therefore in and of itself to have colours and movements before the mind, to have thoughts to the effect: 'This is red; this is moving'. Rather the intentionality of these items (that is, the intentional use of these terms) should incline us to avoid unhelpful expressions like 'a sensation of red', when we mean to be characterizing the content of sensibility. It is indeed implausible to deny that the colour red is the object of someone's awareness, while imputing to him the sensation of it. The expression 'sensation of . . .', despite what philosophers have tried to make of it, retains a strong intentional flavour.

These difficulties aside, the reasons for claiming that sensibility is insufficient for there being something before the mind apply in the same way where one is affected visually, and chromatically, as where one suffers pain or hunger. Sentience, whatever its mode, is not itself intentional.

Let us pause here to take stock of where we are. We began the present chapter with the expectation that Kant would attempt, in the Deduction, to show that the categories are necessary for one's being conscious or aware of anything. We then noted that Kant's argument sets out from the claim that all representations must, if they are to represent anything, or be anything, to me, be capable of being accompanied by the 'I think'. And we tried to show, from the text and from general Kantian grounds, that, contrary to a common interpretation (represented here by Paul Guyer), this thesis does not amount to the claim that for something to be a state of consciousness at all is for it to be self-ascribable. Rather, it is the thesis that *states* of consciousness cannot yield *objects* of consciousness unless they are self-ascribable; in the absence of this condition what is sensorily true *of* one cannot be something that is true *for* one. In the last few pages we have been trying to clarify the distinction between these; and we have been giving reasons as to why, contrary to the doctrine of empiricists, one's being sensorily affected is not sufficient for there being an object of one's consciousness.

We come now, at last, to the question of why it is that Kant believes that if our sensory states are to yield objects for our consciousness, we must be capable of ascribing them to ourselves, accompanying them with the 'I think'. What is supposed to be the crucial point of connection between the notion of an object of the mind and that of the capacity for self-consciousness? Our discussion above already suggests that the first person singular (I) is in some way connected with the idea of an object of consciousness, and that that is a way in which it is not connected with the idea of a state of consciousness. Taking a first-person standpoint on a state of consciousness, we argued, makes it seem as if the mere fact of being in that state involves being aware that one is— which means the same as ascribing it to oneself; and to do that, we claimed, is to make of the state an object of one's awareness. From this it seems to follow that the self-ascription of a representation brings with it, is sufficient for, there being an object of one's consciousness.[11] This may itself be interesting and suggestive, but it is not enough. What we need is, with a modal shift, its converse: the *capacity* for self-ascription of representations is *necessary* for one's being aware of something. (The end result, one might suspect, will in fact be a bi-conditional: I am aware of something in having a representation, if, and only if, I can ascribe the representation to myself.) What argues for this thesis? Why should one not have an object before one's consciousness where, for whatever reason, one is quite incapable of self-ascription? Why should one not simply *see* red (or something red)? Now, I think Guyer is right in claiming that Kant does not himself provide any explicit argument for this. Perhaps he is in a way 'conflating' consciousness of something with the capacity for self-consciousness. (Guyer does not, of course, distinguish consciousness of something from being in a conscious state, having representations. He is quite wrong, as we have argued, in taking Kant to be conflating the *latter* with the capacity for self-consciousness.) But I think such a conflating can be made to seem plausible. Let us rehearse the central distinction. What, again, is supposed to be the difference between an object of consciousness and a state, between being aware of a colour and being merely, as we have put it, chromatically affected? In the latter case, it is simply

---

[11] So long as it really is a case of *self-ascription*. If the first-person utterance functions in some other way (e.g. as a cry, a complaint) then the connection to an object of consciousness will not hold.

true of me that my sensibility contains this element red. In the former, something is *true for me*, namely that this is red. Now, what needs to be made out, if we are to defend Kant's thesis, is that the idea 'true for me', unlike the idea 'true of me', is an essentially first-person idea; that to say that something is true for someone, that he thinks it, is to impute to him the capacity to formulate his thought in first-person terms. In other words, a thought, unlike a state of sentience, is just the sort of thing on which one *must* be able to take a first-person stance. I am not suggesting that this is obvious. Indeed, it might seem sufficient, for purposes of distinguishing a thought (true for him) from a mere state (true of him), that the one who has the thought be able to formulate it in *some* terms. Let it be granted, it might be said, merely to be in a state of sentience (hunger, chromatic affection, etc.) does not require that one formulate anything to oneself, and that to think something, on the other hand, does require it. (Indeed, it consists of it.) But there is no reason to suppose, it will be said, that the formulation of the thought must be in first-person terms; it will be enough for one to have red as the object of one's consciousness that one be able to say to himself: 'It's red', or even, simply, 'red'. Now that is true; but it does not go deep enough. For we need to know what it is in virtue of which the utterance 'red' or 'it's red' is the formulation of his *thought*, of how things are *for him*, as opposed to its being merely, for example, the noise he makes (overtly, or as it were internally) *when chromatically affected*. The fact that some formula occurs in a mind when that mind is affected thus and so does not itself make the formula a thought or the expression of a thought. The utterance 'red', or 'it's red', might have been nothing more than a verbal counterpart to the bull's snorting and charging, an expressing, a venting, of chromatic affection, as 'ouch!' or 'damn!' are expressings or ventings of pain. In such a case the force of 'red' or 'it's red' would be explicated in terms of sensibility alone; no room has been left for that crucial factor of intentionality that characterizes all thought to the effect that so and so, namely the idea of things being thus and so *for* one. The occurrence of words, or thought-elements, in the mind when one is sensorily affected is, then, not sufficient for the words or elements to constitute a thought.

What, then, must we add to the idea of such an occurrence in the mind to make that occurrence a case of a thought, of things being thus and so for one? It is here, I think, that it becomes plausible to say: if things are thus and so for one, then one must be capable of seeing them as *precisely such*, namely as being thus and so *for one*. For where the utterance (say 'red') is not, as in the hypothetical case considered above, forced from one as a cry, but where it constitutes one's spelling out (however briefly and unselfconsciously), how things are for one, then it seems impossible that one should be simply incapable of seeing it as that, *as* spelling out how things are for one. Thinking something to be so, unlike mere sentience, has that intrinsic reflexivity about it. Another way of putting this is to say that whenever one thinks '*p*' one's thought *can* take the form 'I think *p*'. If something could not take that form, it would not be my *thought* (or *my* thought), it would not be a case of my portraying how things are for me. This is equivalent to Kant's formulation: 'It must be possible for the "I think" to accompany all my representations . . . '

We must be careful not to miscast the role of this reflexivity. The requirement that one be capable of ascribing representations to oneself is not the requirement that for any thought '*p*' I have, I must be capable of the further thought: 'I think *p*'. This, in any case, would lead to an infinite regress, since the thought: 'I think *p*', being a thought, is itself of the form '*q*', and would generate the further thought: 'I think *q*'. If the 'I think' is to play the role that Kant assigns to it, that of providing for the very possibility that being in a sensory state should yield a thought about something, then we cannot understand it as itself a thought about something. And, *a fortiori*, it cannot be, what its structure suggests, a thought *about me*. If it were, moreover, I would in having the thought conceive of myself as its subject, and what I thereby conceived would have to be accessible to me, that is, capable of being given in some intuition. Kant is fully aware of these problems. 'The "I" is indeed in all our thoughts, but there is not in this representation the least trace of intuition' (A350). Again, 'the "I think" serves only to introduce (*aufführen*) all our thought, as belonging to consciousness' (A341/B399). I hear this as saying that the 'I think' is nothing more than the very mark (for myself?) of my consciousness of something; it expresses, makes explicit, the fact that something is so *for me*—that *I take it* to be so.

We have considered, now, three interrelated questions concerning Kant's requirement that 'it must be possible for the "I think" to accompany all my representations . . . ': 1. What is the requirement for? (On pain of what must this be possible?); 2. What, if anything, justifies the claim that it is a requirement?; and 3. What does this accompanyability of the 'I think' actually amount to? The view that has emerged from these considerations is this. If, in being sensorily affected, I am to be aware of something, if something is to be thus and so for me and not merely true of my sentient state, then I must be capable of regarding it as such, as a matter of how things are for me. I must be capable of conceiving things *as* belonging to my consciousness.

Let us once again step back for a broader view. We anticipate that Kant will, in the Transcendental Deduction, attempt to prove that there can be no awareness of anything, no grasping of an item in consciousness, without the employment of the categories of the understanding. If, as we suggested earlier, the self-consciousness thesis (the 'I think') is the first step of this argument, then we may expect that a connection will be drawn between the idea of the capacity for self-consciousness on the one hand and that of the employment of the categories on the other. Somehow it must be shown that the only thing that could account for my ability to conceive what is sensorily given as belonging to my consciousness is that I unite the sensory data by performing acts of judgment, and so by employing the categories.

Now this presupposes that my ability to conceive things as objects of my consciousness is problematic and stands in need of some special account, and one might ask why this is. Why should it not simply be *given*, as Descartes seems to have supposed it to be, that we are conscious of what we are conscious of *as* belonging to us? Why shouldn't this reflexivity be a brute fact about consciousness of objects? It is the beginning of an answer to this question to repeat those qualifications on what the 'I think' reveals. That I can prefix 'I think' to any formulation of my consciousness of something does not mean that in being conscious of anything I am also conscious of myself, as if a full inventory of the objects before my mind included that item: *me*. Even the phrase 'conscious of myself simply as conscious being, as pure subject of awareness' will mislead us if it allows us to suppose that we can infer from the 'I think' that I in fact exist as a conscious subject. Kant forbids any such inference. ('We do not have, and cannot have, any knowledge whatever of any such subject' (A350).) Only if the 'I think' were to make a *statement about me* (a statement someone else could make about me by saying 'he thinks') could anything about me be inferred from it (e.g. A362–3). But that is what it does not do. 'I think *p*', as here understood, states no more than does '*p*'; nothing can be inferred from the former that cannot be inferred from the latter. The content of the thought in 'I think *p*' is identical with the content of the thought in '*p*'. But this does not mean that therefore the prefix 'I think' is nothing at all. It 'serves to introduce all our thought as belonging to consciousness'. It makes explicit the fact that any thought I have spells out how things are for me. It is the mark not of self-consciousness, of consciousness of self, but of consciousness of anything. It is the reminder that awareness of something is a state of affairs *for* someone, or *to* someone, not merely in or about someone.

So the 'I think', the for-me factor essential to consciousness of anything, cannot be found within the content, or among the objects, of my consciousness. This is so just because whatever can be found there owes its presence precisely to the fact that it is something *for me*. But this raises the problem of how, then, we are to explain the for-me factor in consciousness. How is it possible the I should be present to myself *purely* as the subject of my awareness—as an item, that is, of which I cannot be conscious, and which, indeed, I cannot conceive as being anything whatever? (For to conceive it as something is to detach it from its role as subject and to make of it an object of my consciousness, which, in being so, would once more be something *for me*.) We cannot understand the presence of myself to myself in my consciousness of anything in the way in which we understand the presence to myself of anything of which I am conscious. How, then, are we to understand it? This question comes to the same as the following: How are we to account for the difference between being in a state of sensibility and being aware of something? We know that the difference can be *marked* by saying that the latter, unlike the former, is something essentially *for me*. But we now also know that that differentiating factor cannot be accounted for by there being, in the case of awareness of something, some additional element or ingredient, an extra piece of furniture in the mind, over and above the data of sense. How, then, are we to account for it? Kant is not obviously wrongheaded in supposing this to be a genuine issue.

What is needed, then, is an exposition, a displaying, of the *means* whereby the data of sensibility become transformed into something for me. Such a means, whatever it turns out to be, must consist in there being set up some relation between those data and the mind on which they are inflicted. The question is: What can that relation be such that the *relata*, once the relation is set up, are on the one hand objects of consciousness, and on the other the subject that is conscious of them? Kant's first move, in pursuing the answer to this question is to remark that the for-me factor, the representation 'I think', 'is an act of *spontaneity*, that is, it cannot be regarded as belonging to sensibility' (B132). He gives no immediate reason for this claim, and it may strike one as yet another barely functioning and indeed distracting architectural item, a further and rather feeble attempt to enforce the high dichotomy of the faculties of Sensibility and Understanding. But I think the claim is a substantive one, and that it performs a crucial role here. There are two points involved. The first is that consciousness of anything is a matter of *action*, something, somehow, that we *do*, not a matter of our being receptive, of taking things in. The second, and more important point, is that such an action is *spontaneous*. This means that it is in no way *grounded* or *based* on the data of sensibility, though it is exerted upon them. It is not, in other words, some sort of reasoned response, a response tailored to the data, as if I acted that way *because* of how things struck me or what they seemed to be like, or in general because of any facts about the data. For if such a grounding or basis in the data were so much as possible, the act would be quite superfluous. If, prior to the performing of that act, things could already strike me or seem to me to be thus and so, if anything could be a fact for me, then the 'I think' would already be there too, and there would be no call for the act that was purportedly to introduce it. But to suppose that the 'I think' is already there, prior to any such act, is to suppose that it is *given* (in inner sense, no doubt) together with other data of sensibility (which, again, is to assume that sensibility alone provides us with understanding). But we know now that the 'I think', the for-me factor, cannot be made sense of by reference to what is given in sensibility, or to the content of the mind.[12] That content can yield only objects of consciousness (and then only when the for-me factor has been provided) never its subject. So if we allow that the for-me

---

[12] Not that Kant never lapses from this insight. At B142, for example, he seems to allow that one could have the thought 'If I support a body, I feel an impression of weight' (though not the thought: 'This body is heavy') simply on the basis of association and without the operation of the necessary unity of apperception. What he should have said, on my reading, is that without the synthesis of apperception I could form no thought whatever with respect to my intuitions—though it would still be the case that I felt an impression of weight when supporting a body. I would like to think that similar revisions apply to the unfortunate distinction, at *Prolegomena* §18, between judgments of

factor cannot be accounted for by reference to the data of sensibility, then we must also allow that the act which introduces it is an ungrounded 'spontaneous' one. It is an act that by its very nature cannot take into consideration how things are.

What sort of act can this be? Given our expectation as to the goal of the Deduction—that its aim is to show that there can be no consciousness of anything without the employment of the categories, that is, without judgment—we have good reason to suspect that the act in question, the 'spontaneous' act which creates (or is) the for-me factor, and so distinguishes consciousness of anything from mere sentience, will ultimately turn out to be the act of judgment. And this will indeed be Kant's conclusion. It is the act of judgment, of judg*ing*, exerted upon the data of sensibility, that makes for consciousness of objects by making it possible that the 'I think' should be capable of accompanying all my representations. But *how* does judging effect this? What is supposed to be the connection between the for-me factor on the one hand and acts of judging on the other, such that only the latter can produce the former?

There is a quick answer to this question, too quick an answer, which runs as follows. For the for-me factor to be present is for something to be thus and so (or true) for me. But something can be thus and so for me only if (and indeed if) I *judge* it to be thus and so. To say that it is true for someone that p is precisely to say that that someone judges that p.[13] The reason that this is too quick as an answer to our question here is that it fails to provide us with any guarantee that judgment (or judging), as here understood, carries with it any, let alone all, of the equipment that is needed. Simply to make plausible the

experience and judgments of perception. What accounts for these lapses is once again Kant's failure to see the necessity for non-first-person criteria for sensibility.

[13] This is why Kant can say that the representation 'I think' is *itself* an act (B132) (ultimately the act of judging), rather than saying merely that it is *made possible* by that act. The act of judging is a sufficient as well as necessary condition of the presence of the for-me factor.

claim that all consciousness of objects, all experience, involves judgment, somehow intuitively understood, will not be sufficient for the purposes in hand. A Locke or a Hume could readily agree that to be aware of something one must conceive it as this or that, red or sweet, and that to do that is to *judge* it to be thus or so, red or sweet. So Kant is not begging any question against the empiricists in claiming merely that consciousness of objects involves thought, or judgment, as such. They could, and should, agree to this. But in doing so they would not, and quite rightly, see themselves as thereby committed to any system of categories.[14] What needs to be shown in the Deduction is that the for-me factor (and therefore all consciousness of objects) necessitates judgment, not just as it might be understood in some general way, but *as it is specified in the Clue*. It must be shown, that is, that the for-me factor requires the functions of unity, those unifying operations of the understanding which, when conceived as having application to objects, are the categories.

And it will not be enough, at this stage in the Deduction, to add to the quick answer a mere appeal to the outcome of the Clue; that is, it will not be enough to supplement the quick answer with the claim that Kant has already shown that judgment involves functions of unity and thus the categories. For that too will beg the central question. As we saw earlier, in Chapter 4, Kant cannot justifiably claim to have demonstrated in the Clue that any thought to the effect that so-and-so, anything that could count as judgment, must involve the categories—as if empiricism were already undermined at that point in the *Critique*. What was demonstrated in the Clue was only that every fully articulated judgment, every thought about anything that finds expression in a declarative sentence—where declarative sentences are known to obey such and such rules—involves the categories. This in no way implies that all judgment—

[14] But it is not as if we have not already begun to argue against such philosophers as these. They would not, I presume, readily agree that the act in question is 'spontaneous', that it cannot be founded on sensibility.

anything that can count as a judgment—must involve the categories, *unless* it is also shown that those rules of declarative sentences are not, for example, arbitrary or conventional or in some other way merely parochial, but that they have their source in the very nature of judgment itself. What has to be shown, to put it in other words, is that the functions of unity, the unifying operations of the understanding, really are essential to judgment (to all cases of judging), and are not merely rules for composing paradigmatic sentences for making assertions in languages like German or English. And to say this is, not surprisingly, to state yet again the central project of the Transcendental Deduction.

So what needs to be argued from the standpoint of the present stage of the inquiry is that the for-me factor requires judgment, *as* judgment is specified in the Clue, that it requires the functions of unity. It needs to be proved that nothing could be thus and so for me unless I employed those functions, unless I unified representations by means of these operations of the understanding. We need, then, a connecting link between the for-me factor on the one hand and functions of unity on the other.

Now Kant thinks he has found this link in the notion of *unity* itself (B130). But not, of course, just any sort of unity. He believes that that unity (of consciousness) that constitutes the for-me factor—the unity that is marked, and displayed, by the fact that the 'I think' can always be appended to any thought—is one and the same unity as is achieved by the functions of unity, those operations of the understanding from which the argument of the analytic began. This will mean that the 'unity' in 'functions of unity', that unique togetherness or coherence which distinguishes a judgment or proposition from a mere list of words or jumble of representations (see Chapter 2), its having a sense or meaning of its own, is nothing other than the unity of consciousness, the for-me factor, itself. There is no question that this is a significant and far-reaching claim. Can it be made out?

Our work towards it must begin at the point, in the

Deduction, that we have reached. We know that we cannot take the for-me factor, the ever-present possibility of appending the 'I think', simply for granted. The fact that whatever I am aware of is thus and so for me, that I am present to myself solely as subject of my awareness,[15] poses a special problem. *How* can I be present to myself in this unique sort of way, a way which disallows the possibility that I should in any way be an object or part of the content of my awareness? How can we make sense of the for-me factor, given its universality and necessarily subjective character? We need a new model, a new picture, for the involvement of the self in consciousness —one that is crucially different from both Descartes's and Hume's.

It is a first step, and one taken in the right direction, to say that consciousness (apperception) is 'spontaneous', or 'original', not derivative from what is given. Kant's second step is a bold one: apperception, that act which makes it possible always to append the 'I think', is an act of *synthesis* or *combination*. And Kant has a way of explaining this. The availability of the 'I think' in all consciousness is what he calls the 'analytic unity of consciousness', or of apperception. To say that it is always possible for the 'I think' to accompany all my representations . . . is to say that I can, as it were, *analyse out* one and the same self, as the common subject of awareness, from every case of my awareness of anything. But all analysis presupposes synthesis (B130), and 'the analytic unity of apperception is possible only under the presupposition of a certain *synthetic* unity' (B133). That is: 'Only in so far as I can unite a manifold of given representations in *one consciousness*, is it possible for me to represent to myself the *identity of the consciousness in these representations*' (ibid.). So the act that makes it possible for me to abstract or analyse out the common subject of all my awareness is that of synthesizing or uniting the representations 'in one consciousness'.

Before we directly consider how this talk about

[15] In so far as I am *necessarily* present to myself. We are not here speaking of *empirical* self-consciousness.

synthesis might lead us to our goal (of identifying the act that makes possible the 'I think' as the act of judgment by means of the categories) we should ask two questions. First, why is it supposed that all analysis presupposes synthesis (as a spontaneous act)? Secondly (and the importance of this will be clear in a moment), are there generically different acts of synthesis, underlying, respectively, the various different types of analysis that are possible? Is it the case, for example, that whereas synthesizing 'in one consciousness' is the act underlying our ability to analyse out the common subject of awareness, some other act of synthesis underlies our capacity to analyse out *red*, say, as the property common to these and those objects of awareness? We might learn something with regard to the former of these questions by first considering the latter.

I think Kant needs to hold (and does hold, as we shall see in a moment) that there are *not* generically different acts of synthesis. If the synthesis that makes it possible to abstract the common subject of awareness were a different act than that which makes it possible to abstract a common object, or common feature of objects, of awareness, then the all-important identity between the presence of the for-me factor and there being objects of consciousness at all would be destroyed. There would be one account of how there can be objects of *my* consciousness, and another account of how there can be *objects* of my consciousness. If my being conscious *of* anything (e.g. red) *is* for things to be thus and so *for me*, then whatever accounts for the one must account for the other. There is, after all, only one state of affairs, not two or several, to be accounted for. If 'synthesizing in one consciousness' is the act that enables me to abstract the common subject of consciousness, then it must also be the act that enables me to abstract red, or anything else, as what is common to objects of consciousness.

And Kant does indeed declare that the act of synthesis is 'originally one' thing (*ursprünglich einig*) and 'amounting to the same (*gleichgeltend*) for all combination'

(B130).[16] And that theme is interestingly elaborated in a revealing footnote to B133; which is worth quoting in full:

The analytic unity of consciousness belongs to all general concepts, as such. If, for instance, I think red in general, I thereby represent to myself a property which (as a characteristic) can be found in something, or can be combined with other representations; that is, only by means of a presupposed possible synthetic unity can I represent to myself the analytic unity. A representation which is to be thought as common to *different* representations is regarded as belonging to such as have, in addition to it, also something *different*. Consequently it must previously be thought in synthetic unity with other (though, it may be, only possible) representations, before I can think in it the analytic unity of consciousness, which makes it a *conceptus communis*. The synthetic unity of apperception is therefore that highest point, to which we must ascribe all employment of the understanding, even the whole of logic, and conformably therewith, transcendental philosophy. Indeed this faculty of apperception is the understanding itself.

This remark, singularly misplaced as a footnote, tells us important things about why analysis presupposes synthesis; about how it is that synthesis is *einig* and *gleichgeltend* for all combination (which means as we shall see, about the relation of *concepts* to *consciousness*); and about what all this has to do with the nature of understanding as such.

One might at first think that the talk about the concept *red* here is meant somehow to be *analogous* to the talk about the concept of the self. As if Kant were giving some sort of analogical explanation of the unity of consciousness, perhaps as follows: just as a common

[16] Why the qualification 'originally' (or perhaps 'fundamentally')? I think because there are, after all, different *functions* of unity—different ways or methods, if you wish, of performing the selfsame act of uniting representations in one consciousness. I do not think it is necessary or profitable to quibble about whether we should speak of one act here or of many. The point is that to synthesize—by whichever of the twelve functions—is always to unite representations in one consciousness, to do which is to bring about the synthetic unity of apperception.

feature in experience, like red, is abstractible from the manifold, so the common subject of experience, the self, is abstractible from it (analytic unity of consciousness); and just as the former capacity to abstract requires a prior act of synthesis, so also does the latter (synthetic unity of apperception). I do not believe that this is what Kant is doing here. He is not comparing the unity in a concept (analytic or synthetic) with the unity (analytic or synthetic) in the self; he is identifying them. The analytic unity of consciousness, concerning which the note begins, is not, as we might have thought, exhausted in the one-sided idea of the abstractible common subject of consciousness. It (there is only one such) is present in ('belongs to') every concept, every general idea. Indeed, to be a general idea at all is to embody the analytic unity of consciousness; it is what 'makes it a *conceptus communis*'.

What this amounts to is, I think, this. For something to be a general concept, like *red*, is for it to be, or mean, the same to me (to the person for whom it is a concept) in all its various applications. And to say that is to say that it embodies an identity, or unity, of consciousness through all the variety of different representations in which it is embedded. To be a concept is precisely to do that.[17]

Now at this point it might perhaps still look as if Kant is employing two different and parallel notions of (analytic) unity, or identity, of consciousness. There is the notion of 'same consciousness' on the one hand as it is present in the 'I think', and on the other as it is present in every general concept. It is important to see that this is not so. A general concept *embodies*, as we have chosen to put it, the analytic unity of consciousness: *red* is, or means, one and the same thing to me, whether it is that apple, this ball or some flag that I am taking to be red. The 'I think', on the other hand, does not embody such unity. The claim is not that the *I* (of apperception) is or means the same *to me*, in all the variety of representa-

<hr />

[17] See also the note to B136, where Kant explains a concept, as opposed to an intuition, as 'that through which one and the same consciousness is found to be contained in a number of representations'. And also A103.

tions accompanying it. (That would yield our infinite regress once again.) The 'I think' (which, after all, is no more than the 'to me', or 'for me') is merely the *mark* of the unity of consciousness; it *displays* it without containing or embodying it in any way. It is the formula we employ in showing what a concept is, in showing how it is that a concept embodies the analytic unity of consciousness: *red* means the same to me . . . So it is not as if there is one (analytic) unity in the self of apperception, and other in concepts, like *red*. There is only one, and it is exemplified in the general concept *red*, in the fact that 'red' means the same to me in all the variety of combinations in which it occurs.

Now whatever connection between concepts and consciousness is adumbrated here, it is as yet only, as Kant would say, on the 'analytic' level. We have learned that unity in a concept and unity of consciousness are one and the same thing. This, by itself, is only a stage on the way to an answer to our question of how the for-me factor is possible. We wish to discover how it is that, what makes it possible that, I should be ˙present to myself as non-objectifiable subject of my awareness. We do not yet discover this by being told that such presence is embodied in, and only in,[18] the possession of any general concept. We need to answer a further question, that of how general concepts are possible. What explains the fact that 'red', for example, means something to me, one and the same thing in all its occurrences? And of course not just any answer to this question will do. We need an account of general concepts which *explains* and does not *take for granted* the unity of consciousness embodied in them; we need an account which at one and the same time generates both concepts and unity of consciousness. Thus, an abstractionist account of concepts will not do. One could not note that in all these different situations there was a common feature, or that things were 'resembling', or whatever, unless unity of consciousness

[18] Intuitions, being blind *per se*, cannot embody the for-me factor, and it, the for-me factor, needs embodiment, being by itself nothing at all. We shall soon see more clearly just why concepts exclusively can do the job.

were already present in the awareness of things in those
situations, that is unless such unity were present prior to
the having of a concept. But if this were so, no attention
to the source of concepts would be relevant to explaining
unity of consciousness. What kind of account of concepts
will also be an account of unity of consciousness, of the
for-me factor?

It is in response to this question that Kant speaks, in
the note to B133, of *synthetic* unity. To 'think red in
general', to entertain the idea red (where that idea
embodies the analytic unity of consciousness), is to
represent to oneself something which can be found here
and there (*irgend woran angetroffen*), as, essentially as, a
characteristic of something (a ball, an apple). And to
think of red as essentially a characteristic of something is
to regard it as essentially *combinable* with other representations. (And combinable in, of course, a specific way
—the way in which things are combined when something is a characteristic of something.) Apart from such
combinability, there is no concept red, no analytic unity
of consciousness is embodied here, there is no such thing
as anything's being red for me. And so 'only by means of a
presupposed possible synthetic unity can I represent to
myself the analytic unity.' What Kant is claiming here is
that the representation red (or any other) cannot constitute a concept, cannot be or mean anything to me, cannot
be accompanied by the 'I think', unless it is conceived by
me as combinable with other representations. Neither
red nor anything else can mean anything to me as it were
atomistically—simply in virtue of its being a representation in me. Without such conceived combinability the
representation remains a datum of sensibility, a mere
chromatic affection. But how is combinability conceived? What is it for a representation to be 'thought in
synthetic unity' with other representations? Kant's answer is plain. I can think red as combinable with other
representations in the way it must be thought if it is to be
conceived as a characteristic *only if* I can myself perform
such combinatory acts, only if I can put together the
thought that this or that is red. If I could not do this, if I

could not fashion the judgment that this or that is red, if I could not, in other words, predicate red of things, then I could not have the concept red, that representation 'would be nothing to me'. So analysis presupposes synthesis, or, and this is the same point, the having of concepts presupposes the capacity to make judgments.

Let us weigh anchor once more and take our bearings again. Do we now have the ingredients necessary for making the connection we have so long been seeking between judgment by means of the categories and the forme factor, or consciousness of anything? If what we have been saying above is true, and supported by Kant's argument, and generalizable to all possible representations, then perhaps the prospect is hopeful. If it is true that the representation, the chromatic affection, red cannot be anything to me unless I synthesize it with other representations in such a way as to predicate red of something, then it seems clear that I must employ at least the categorical (subject-predicate) function of unity. And if this function, then surely also the others. I could hardly be capable of predicating red of anything unless I could also quantify (*a*, or this, is red, everything is red, some things are red), assert or deny (*is* red, is *not* red), and modalize (is actually red, might be, must be, red). And if similar things are true of all other representations (and why shouldn't they be?—red, after all, was quite randomly picked) then it seems that we have reached our goal: there can be no consciousness of anything, nothing can be or mean anything to one, unless one employs the functions of unity, unless one judges by means of the categories.

Unfortunately, however, this strategy is not open to Kant, and it is instructive to see why it is not. The talk about red, or any such talk about some specific concept, can do no more than illustrate a thesis whose proof must come from elsewhere.[19] It has *not* been shown that the datum, the chromatic affection, red cannot be anything to me, unless it is synthesized with other data *in such a*

[19] This, I imagine, is the explanation of why the talk about red occurs in a footnote rather than in the main text.

way as to be predicated of something. Of course the *term*
'red' is a predicate; that is how we do in fact operate with
it. But to say that is not yet to say that only when we
operate with it in that way will red (the chromatic
affection) be anything to us. A case has perhaps been
made for the claim that *some* sort of synthesis or putting
together is necessary—we shall look at this possibility
more closely below—but no argument we have considered does anything to show that only that kind of
synthesis which is reflected in the structure of actual
declarative sentences will do the job. It may, in other
words, be plausible to say that some unifying operations
must be at work if there is to be consciousness of
anything, but why there should be just these, the ones
that lie so conveniently 'ready at hand' in the language
we happen to have, has not been revealed. And it will not
do to say at this point that these, the 'functions of unity
in judgment', are the only ones (or the most basic ones)
there are, that they 'specify the understanding completely, and yield an exhaustive inventory of its powers'.
This, as we have repeatedly seen, is just what needs to be
shown. We still have not been given reasons for supposing that just these modes of synthesis are necessary for
consciousness.

But now it might occur to one that we are asking too
much of the Transcendental Deduction. Commentators
frequently point out that the Deduction argues for the
indispensability, not of *the* categories, that particular set
of twelve arrived at in the Clue, but simply of *categories*,
where it is assumed that we know which ones they are.
And this is surely true; the argument of the Deduction
barely mentions, and certainly does not depend on any
mention of, the individual categories or functions of
unity; and this is not a failing of any sort on the part of
the Deduction. The individual categories are, after all,
subsequently 'deduced' in the Principles. So we should
expect a certain openness in the conclusion reached in
the Deduction.

But there are definite limits to this openness. What
cannot be left undecided is the question of what, in

general, is to *count* as synthesis, as the relevant kind of putting together; whether, for example, only some linguistic operation, like predicating or hypothesizing, will suffice, or whether some quite other kind of putting together will do, a kind, perhaps, that varies from individual to individual or from occasion to occasion; and why not call it 'judgment'? (Kant does have something to say about this, though not enough, as we shall see.) What, I think, the Deduction must show if it is to be successful is that there could be no for-me factor, no consciousness of anything, if one did not synthesize the representations *by those operations which are reflected in the structure of the (public) language, whatever those operations might be.* This last clause gives the requisite openness; we would not expect the Deduction to argue that one must, in particular, predicate or quantify. But the restriction to operations-reflected-in-the-language is crucial. It must not seem to be an accident that those and only those operations which are discoverable by contemplating the structure of our language are necessary for consciousness of anything. Why should there not be alternative modes of synthesis, quite independent of our language, which equally well yield the for-me factor? What is needed is a general argument connecting the for-me factor not just with *synthesis* but with *language*. Does Kant in fact have such an argument?

In the Deduction there are of course some important restrictions on what can count as synthesis, restrictions which stem from the peculiarities of the for-me factor; and it is here that we should look for the seeds of such an argument. The for-me factor cannot be taken for granted, as we have seen. The fact that representations represent, that the data of sensibility mean something to me, cannot be accounted for with reference to those data. The data must somehow be brought to consciousness, and, indeed, to that focal point, the unity of consciousness. And that result cannot be achieved, as Kant says, 'simply through my accompanying each representation with consciousness' (B133). To suppose that it can is to think of consciousness, the for-me factor, as another entity in the field, complete unto itself, as it were, something which could, but need not, go together with something else. But consciousness, in the relevant sense, that which distinguishes something's meaning something to me from mere sentience, is as we have repeatedly seen, something essentially incomplete; it is not something independently identifiable, like a roving eye (with a built-in mirror), which needs only to light upon (accompany) an item to yield awareness of an object.[20]

But if the for-me factor cannot be introduced by being added to the data of sensibility, how can it be introduced? 'Only', says Kant, immediately following the passage just quoted, 'in so far as I *conjoin* (*hinzusetze*) one representation with another, and am aware of the synthesis of them' (B133). Why only thus? No argument is offered at this point. But perhaps we can construct one out of ideas already available. On the one hand, representations, the data of sensibility, do not, singly or in groups, constitute consciousness—they cannot account for the for-me factor. Consciousness is something additional, supervenient, to them, it is 'spontaneous'. But, on the other hand, representations cannot come to constitute consciousness by having an 'I think', a for-me factor, *materially added* to them. Consciousness is not in *that* way something additional, it has no life of its own apart from representations. But what possibility is now left? Something must be done to the data of sensibility which makes of them something more than data of sensibility, without however adding anything to them. The change must be, as Kant would say, a formal one—a matter of arranging rather than one of materially adding. And if the result is to mean something to me, I must put the data together, one with another, in such a way that I am conscious of the whole that is thereby produced.[21] So

[20] This would be to make *analytic* unity basic. The 'I think' does indeed *accompany* representations—i.e. I can analyse it out. The mistake is to think that it got there in the first place in the same sort of way, only back to front: just as I can *pick it out* from this set of representations, so it originally came to be there by being *placed among them*. Synthesis is not analysis-in-reverse.

[21] This, I think, is what Kant means by saying, in B133, 'I am conscious of the synthesis of them (the representations)'. He is *not* saying that my act of synthesis is the object of my consciousness!

much is plausibly suggested, if not exactly entailed, by the fact that the for-me factor is itself something essentially incomplete. The difference between my being in a sentient state and something's meaning something to me cannot consist in the presence, in the latter case, of an additional element. But if that is so, if there is no difference, so to speak, in the number of items present, then the required difference must somehow consist in how those items are arranged. Only a putting together of data, a conjoining one with another (in consciousness) can yield a 'for-me'. So there is an argument to the effect that synthesis is necessary for consciousness.

Now *language* seems to fit this bill of synthesis rather nicely. In asserting that something is so by uttering a declarative sentence we do in fact put items together in such a way that the result is thus and so for me (for the one who utters). And the difference between a mere list of words which asserts nothing and a sentence which yields a statement is not that the latter contains a constituent lacking in the former; it is a matter, quite clearly, of how the words are put together. So language (statement-making) provides us with a good *model* for the synthesis that is to make possible the for-me factor. But of course this is not enough. What needs to be shown is not that language will fit the bill, but that *only* language will fit the bill; that only those acts the performance of which produces coherent sentences out of mere lists (compare 'manifolds') of words can yield a for-me. But showing that requires that we answer the question of *why* only those operations which are displayed in the structure of the public language can yield the for-me factor. What is it that argues that the unity or sense produced by the synthesizing act be *communicable*? Why shouldn't that unity or sense be an essentially *subjective, private* one? This is a possibility that Kant must be in a position to dismiss if he is to show that judgment by means of the categories is necessary for any such sense or unity—if, in other words, the Deduction is to succeed. I believe that there is a level on which Kant can dismiss this possibility, and that there is another level on which he cannot.

There are, prima facie, two distinguishable aspects to the 'publicness', the non-privacy, of language. There is, first, the fact that language is a *social* phenomenon; one speaks, another responds. We talk with one another, and to be understood by one another, and our utterances belong together, and with other actions of ours, in a complex social fabric. Secondly, there is the fact that how I speak is, in another way, not simply my private concern. Whether my utterance succeeds in making a statement (or asking a question, or whatever, whether it is intelligible at all), is not a subjective matter, up to me to decide. (Nor, of course, is it up to the community to decide, say by majority vote!) The criteria for making sense are objective, not subject to arbitrary decision; language is *rule-governed*. So our language is on the one hand a social phenomenon, on the other a rule-governed one.

This, I should stress, is a prima-facie distinction; I do not mean to be suggesting that these features are ultimately distinct or that either could in fact exist apart from the other. That is a question I leave open for the time being. But whether or not these two aspects of language are ultimately distinct, it is certainly possible, in philosophy, to pay attention to the one while more or less ignoring the other. It is noteworthy that where Locke, for example, initially, at least, emphasizes the social aspect of language to the neglect of its rule-governedness, Kant does the opposite. While scarcely noting the fact that people speak to one another, he is insistent, both in the Deduction and in the Clue, on the fact that anything that is to count as judgment is governed by fixed rules. We will see later how this one-sidedness affects the outcome of the Deduction. In the meantime it is worth seeing that Kant does in fact have, in what we have already considered, an argument to the effect that only a rule-governed synthesis could possibly yield a situation in which things are thus and so for me.

The argument stems from the notion of spontaneity. To say that the act of synthesis, which is to introduce the for-me factor, must be spontaneous is to say that it cannot be grounded in the data of sensibility; it cannot be tailored to the data, as some sort of reasoned, or otherwise conscious, response to them. To suppose that it could be grounded in such a way as this is to fail to recognize the depth at which the act operates. For if how I synthesized was based on how I was affected in receiving the data, then my being thus affected must have already constituted things being thus and so for me —to suppose which is to presuppose what is in question, it is to ground the act of synthesis in what alone was to have made it possible. Now the reasons for saying that synthesis cannot be grounded in sensibility, if it is to be responsible for the for-me factor, are reasons for saying that it cannot rest on any grounds at all. It is not as if, somehow, *only* sensibility were being ruled out and as if some other sort of grounding were still possible. Whatever introduces the for-me factor must, by its very nature, be the *first*, Kant calls it the 'original' (e.g. B132), act of the understanding. It cannot be, then, that I put the representations together as I please, or because it seems right this way, or better this way than that, or, in short, because of anything.[22] How I synthesize the data can in no way be in my hands or up to me, it cannot be any sort of personal or subjective matter. (Nor, on the other hand, can synthesis be left to chance, as if just any kind of grouping of data would do. If the reception of data *per se* does not explain how things can be thus and so for me, then the same will be true of the reception of any arbitrary collections of data.) Synthesis, if it is to play the role assigned to it, must be an autonomous and objective affair. The putting together that results in a thought, in contradistinction to a jumble of representations, must be governed by fixed rules, and by such rules as distinguish a thought from a jumble. (This is not to say that synthesis is *grounded in a recognition* of the rules, as if I synthesized as I do because these are the rules. That would again be to put the cart before the horse. The rules

---

[22] This is of course not to deny that synthesis is *caused*. It is 'first' *qua* act of the understanding; i.e. it is not grounded in anything *which I take to be so.*

can be recognized only *post facto*, on analysis of what alone can count as a thought.)

It is important to see how this argument fits into the scheme. It is not an argument to the effect that *language* is rule-governed. That is something that in the present context is being taken for granted. The goal of the Deduction is, after all, to show that only the functions of unity specified in the Clue, only the sense-making operations of the public rule-governed language, can be satisfactory candidates for the synthesis that is ·to introduce the for-me factor. What is argued for above is that *anything that is to count as synthesis* must be rule-governed. And that argument, it is worth noting, pays no attention to the findings of the Clue; it is not as if some covert appeal were being made to the fact that there are rules for the formation of declarative sentences. Any such appeal to the fact that sentences are rule-governed would presume what is at issue and so invalidate the attempt to show that only sentential operations can produce the for-me factor (the unity of apperception). The requirement that synthesis be objective and rule-governed is derived exclusively from considerations about the nature of apperception. So whatever else is going on in this argument no question is being begged as to the suitability of the rules of the public language for performing acts of synthesis. We know that synthesis must be rule-governed quite independently of knowing that sentences are rule-governed.

So Kant does have an argument against privacy. The spontaneity of apperception precludes the possibility that synthesis be up to me or that it vary from individual to individual. If synthesis is to make possible, and not itself to presuppose, that things are thus and so for me, then it must be a determinate and autonomous affair, not contingent upon any factors peculiar to me or my situation.

And now it might seem that if we grant everything to this point, the goal of the Deduction is virtually assured. If sensibility, the reception of sense-data, is itself insufficient for awareness of anything, and if that which is

missing in sensibility—that things are thus and so for me
—can be supplied only in acts of synthesizing the data,
where such acts are necessarily spontaneous and therefore rule-governed, *then* it will seem that the public
language provides not only a good model for synthesis,
but the only available model. For what else, one might
ask, but the thought-operations expressed in how we
speak can we point to as exemplifying what is needed, a
rule-governed state-of-affairs-for-me? It is not only that
other models do not readily present themselves, but that
we would be hard put to conceive of something that fits
our requirements that is not itself one or another variant
of the public language. If this is so, then the capacity to
perform those judgmental acts which are expressed in the
public language is not only sufficient for awareness of
something, but also, it seems, necessary for it. And this is
what the Deduction was meant to demonstrate.

Now I think it is probably true that the public language
provides the only available model for synthesis. Once it
has been shown that no 'private', or arbitrary, putting
together of representations could account for the for-me
factor, it no longer seems as if there could be an eligible
rival, as a model for synthesis, to those acts the
performance of which renders what would otherwise be a
mere list into a sentence. It is not as if we have at hand
alternative models for putting items together, in a
rule-governed way, such that the result yields a for-me
situation. Let us allow then, without further argument,
that only the public language exemplifies synthesis.
This, however, still does not yield the desired conclusion
of the Deduction (of that part of the Deduction with
which we are concerned). What Kant needs to show, as
we noted earlier, is that there could be no for-me factor,
no consciousness of anything, if one did not synthesize
the representations by those operations which are reflected in the structure of the public language (whatever
those operations might be). To show this is to show more
than that only those operations exemplify, or provide a
model for, the synthesis that generates the for-me factor.
We are allowing that the public language provides the

only available vehicle for synthesis. This invites the question as to *why this is so*. Why should it be that language, that socially communicating, mutually comprehensible something, should be the only vehicle for fashioning a thought, for thinking? What has thinking, things being thus and so for me, consciousness of anything, got to do with interpersonal communicability, mutual comprehensibility? Why should the ways in which we speak to one another—even allowing that they may be the only possible ways in which beings such as we can speak to one another—dictate what is to count as mere, solitary, thinking? The demon of privacy is popping up again, in a new place. The argument to this point has indeed achieved something; it has deprived us of what might otherwise have been a model for such solitary thinking, namely a putting things together as they strike me, or as I please. The putting together must, it has been argued, be spontaneous, and so rule-governed, it can in no way depend on circumstances or be up to me. So synthesis, consciousness, thinking, is not in *that* sense a private matter. But it does not follow from this that it is therefore *essentially communicable*, that what counts as a thought is somehow socially determined; that what cannot be understood by others is not a thought at all. We need to connect consciousness and communicability. Kant has shown, we have allowed, that only a rule-governed act can yield the for-me factor. What he still needs to show is that only an interpersonally communicable act can be rule-governed in the requisite way. I do not believe he can show this. The idea of communicability is quite foreign to that of synthesis, and there is nothing that allows the two items to be brought together.

But again it might be thought that we are asking too much of Kant's argument. Why can't one simply *derive* communicability from rule-governedness? If the act that creates the for-me factor is neither arbitrarily or idiosyncratically up to me, nor at the mercy of whatever happens to be present to me in intuition, but is altogether independent of anything that is peculiar to me or to my situation, then there is nothing to stand in the way of the communicability, or mutual comprehensibility, of the act.[23] As far as synthesis is concerned there are no differences between people; everybody, every being with a discursive understanding, is in the same position. There is, then, no room at this level for a breakdown in communication.

But this puts the issue of communicability on the wrong footing. We are not concerned with the simple dichotomy: is synthesis (consciousness, thinking), given its rule-governedness, 'public' and communicable on the one hand, or 'private' and incommunicable on the other? If that were our choice the objection above would no doubt be right. But our question is, rather, how does the idea of communicability, or incommunicability, come into the picture at all? Where does any such reference to other people come in? Are we to assume in advance of any argument that if there is to be a being who synthesizes his data in a rule-governed way he must be, and perhaps must regard himself as, one among other such (potential) beings, where the question of communication with these beings must necessarily arise? This may indeed be the case, but it is surely something that calls for some sort of argument or explanation. But there is, as far as I can see, nothing in Kant's characterization of the requirements of synthesis that entails anything about communication, or anything *social* at all.

To be sure of this, let us briefly review the main stages of Kant's argument, as we have presented it. The receiving of sensory data is in itself insufficient for being aware of something, for no such receiving explains what it is for things to be thus and so for one (the analytic unity of consciousness). For things to be thus and so for one requires, in turn, that the data be synthesized in one consciousness, where such synthesis is in no way grounded on the data, and is therefore 'spontaneous', and

---

[23] Kant in fact manœuvres in just this way elsewhere when he argues that the universality of judgments of beauty is deducible from their disinterestedness (see *Critique of Judgement*, trans. J. C. Meredith (Oxford, 1928), Book I, §6).

hence rule-governed. There is nothing, I think, in any of this that requires so much as the possibility of a society of mutually comprehending beings.

Now this again may seem unfair to Kant. If I am capable of seeing things as being thus and so for me, it might be claimed, must I not also be capable of seeing things as being thus and so for someone else? If 'for me', or 'I think' is to mean anything to me (!) I must surely be able and prepared to acknowledge other subjects of consciousness . . .[24] This, even if true, does not obviously imply that I must be, or must regard myself as being, capable of communicating with other such subjects. But much more important for our purposes, this is an argument which Kant could not employ. It perverts the 'I think', the for-me factor, and makes it incapable of performing its role. To say that for me to be conscious of anything is for things to be thus and so for me is *not* to say that a conception of myself as subject enters into my awareness of anything. This would lead again to the infinite regress that we noted before—it is not that 'I think' ('for me') means something *to me*. Unlike Strawson's 'I', the 'I' in the Kantian 'I think' (or the 'me' in 'for me') is not functioning as an identifying pronoun, it does not refer to or pick out anyone. So Kant could not accept an argument from the notion of a conscious and self-conscious subject to some allegedly presupposed notion of other subjects of the same kind. There is in the Transcendental Deduction no such notion of a conscious and self-conscious subject from which such an argument could proceed.

There is, then, nowhere in the argument for the necessity of synthesis for the notion of mutual comprehensibility to find a foothold. There is nothing in the argument even to suggest such an idea. If I am right about this, the Transcendental Deduction of the categories cannot succeed, for the final crucial connection will not have been made; it will not have been shown that only in judging by means of the categories—that is by the rules

[24] Cf. Strawson, *Individuals*, ch. 3.

of the language in which we speak to one another—can
one be aware of anything. But nothing short of this is
Kant's goal.

Before we consider this, and its implications, further,
let us briefly see how Kant in fact executes this crucial
connection in the Deduction. Having established, in the
second edition version, that apperception, consciousness
of anything, is spontaneous, rule-governed, not subject-
ively determined, he turns his attention to the notion of
judgment, expresses dissatisfaction with the prevailing
view as to its nature ('the representation of a relation
between two concepts') and announces:

But if I investigate more precisely the relation of the given
cognitions (*Erkenntnisse*) in any judgment, and distinguish it,
as belonging to the understanding, from the relation according
to laws of the reproductive imagination, which has only
subjective validity, I find that a judgment is nothing but the
manner in which given cognitions are brought to the objective
unity of apperception. (§19,B141)

And two pages later, referring back to this passage, he
says:

But that act of understanding by which the manifold of given
representations (be they intuitions or concepts) is brought
under one apperception, is the logical function of judgment (cf.
§19). All the manifold, therefore, so far as it is given in a single
empirical intuition, is *determined* in respect of one of the
logical functions of judgment, and is thereby brought into one
consciousness. (§20,B143)

And quickly concludes:

Now the *categories* are just these functions of judgment in so
far as they are employed in determination of the manifold of a
given intuition (cf. §13) [i.e. the Clue]. Consequently, the
manifold in a given intuition is necessarily subject to the
categories (ibid.).

I believe this argument is invalid. In the first quoted
passage, from B141, Kant is saying that if one considers
the relation of terms to one another in a judgment, not
from the point of view of whatever ways such a pair or

group of terms might be associated for one, but from the
standpoint of its *being* a judgment, something with a
sense, the expression of a coherent thought, then one will
find that to make a judgment is precisely to put items
together in such a way that the result is a situation for
one.[25] And in looking back on this remark, two pages
later (B143), Kant takes it to imply that it is not merely
judgment as such, but the logical function of judgment,
that produces apperception. From this point the rest is
easy; for the logical function of judgment when thought
of as uniting not merely the terms of the judgment but a
manifold of data, are nothing but the categories. The
categories are therefore involved whenever one is aware
of anything, whenever the manifold is 'brought into one
consciousness' (ibid.).

There is, first, a question about the *direction* of this
argument. We are looking for a process of reasoning *from*
the idea of apperception, consciousness of anything, *to*
the idea of judgment by means of the categories. For what
is needed is a demonstration that only judgment by
means of the categories can effect consciousness of
anything. Yet this argument of Kant's (the only relevant
one in the second edition) begins, unpromisingly, with an
analysis of the idea of judgment. And so it might seem
that the most it could show would be that judgment by
means of the categories brings about apperception—
without showing that apperception is possible *only* by
such means.

But perhaps this difficulty with Kant's argument can
be overcome. It is plausible to see the real direction of the
argument as the opposite of the apparent one. This would
be to see Kant not as claiming that to judge is to unite
data into the consciousness of something—when there
might, for all we know, be ways, other than judging, of
achieving the same result—but as claiming that to judge
is precisely to perform that act we have been interested
in all along, that of uniting data into the consciousness of

[25] Kant's talk about judgment being 'nothing but the *manner* in which . . .'
is, I take it, a reference to there being various forms of judgment. Thus, '*S* is *P*'
puts items together in a different manner than does 'If *P*, then *Q*'.

something. That, the synthesis of apperception, is the real starting point, and the argument identifies it with judgment, and judgment is then unpacked to reveal the categories.

A much more serious difficulty has to do with how we are to understand that identification of synthesis and judgment, as it is introduced in B141. It can be taken in two ways. One of these ways is innocuous, but does not yield the conclusion that apperception involves the categories. The other way licenses the conclusion, but is question-begging on the crucial issue of what judgment involves.

There is nothing untoward about identifying the synthesis of apperception and judgment simply as such. For things to be thus and so for one is for one to think, and why not equally to judge?—that so-and-so. It might even be useful, for appreciating the scope of Kant's thesis, to employ a variety of different expressions here. But, of course, the notion of judgment here employed does not carry any baggage that is not also carried by the notions of apperception, thinking, etc. with which it is being identified. A dyed-in-the-wool empiricist might well agree: to be conscious of red is to think or judge that this something is red. This is simply an alternative terminology and does not take us a step further argumentatively.

But Kant clearly means the identification of apperception and judgment to be much more than an alternative characterization. For he moves rapidly from this identification to the categories; apperception is judgment, and to judge is to utilize logical functions, which, when thought of as structuring a manifold of data (see Chapter 2, above), are the categories (B143). Kant takes it, evidently, that his identification of apperception and judgment entitles him to bring in, as already established, the findings of the Clue as to the nature and conditions of judgment. But this, as we have now twice observed (in Chapter 4, and again in the present chapter, the 'quick answer'), is a serious mistake. The Clue did not establish that the categories are involved in anything that could count as judgment (as if Hume were refuted at that point in the *Critique*). It established only that in our language, our declarative sentences, we portray things in certain ways, as falling under certain rules, the categories. That these same rules are requisite for one's (solitarily) thinking, or judging, anything to be anything cannot be taken as given; it is precisely what the Transcendental Deduction of the categories was designed to show.

It is as if the notion of judgment provides for Kant the crucial link which allows him to identify as one and the same the two great rule-governed systems, public language on the one hand and solitary consciousness on the other—systems which, to this point in the *Critique*, have been investigated independently of each other, the former in the Clue, the latter in the Deduction. But the fact is not that a connecting link has been revealed, but only that we can quite naturally speak of judgment (or thought), with respect to both systems. We can say that to utter the words 'The dog is black' is (paradigmatically or normally) to express the thought, or to judge, that the dog is black. And we can also say that for things to be thus and so for one, when chromatically affected in such and such ways, is for one to judge, or think, for example that the dog is black. But this means only that there is *an* important relationship between speaking and consciousness. And of course there is such a relationship, one that no-one would deny: our language expresses (reflects, conveys, records) our awareness. This relationship is quite sufficient to account for the naturalness of speaking of *judgment* on both sides of the divide, but it is, as such, only a one-way relationship. Language is clearly dependent on consciousness; that alone tells us nothing about there being any sort of reverse dependence.

Let us now pull the strands of the present phase of our investigation together. The goal of the Transcendental Deduction is to show that there can be no consciousness of anything, nothing can be anything for one, unless one synthesizes the data of intuition by means of the categories of the understanding. This means that Kant must show not only that such consciousness, intentional consciousness, requires a synthesis of data, and indeed, a rule-governed synthesis, but also that the rules of that synthesis be identical with those logical rules that govern the formation of coherent declarative sentences. That, in turn, means that Kant must show that one cannot be conscious of something unless one unites the data presented in intuition by those very rules that permit the communicability, the mutual comprehensibility, of that of which one is conscious. But there is nothing, we argued, in Kant's account of the nature and necessity of synthesis that allows for a transition to the rules governing communication, that is the categories. And, we argued finally, the way in which Kant in fact attempts to make the transition begs the question at issue.

But now we find Kant in very much the same situation as that in which we found him at the end of Chapter 2, with respect to the connection of category and schema. He is once again unable to articulate the intimate connection, which he knows must exist, between items which he is constrained to represent as distinct from one another. In both cases Kant has powerful reasons for representing the items in question as distinct. Category and schema, he is convinced, cannot appear in a single unified account of what it is to think about anything, without compromising the very possibility of thinking. Equally, he sees no way in which intentional consciousness and language could be explained together in a unified theory without assuming what needs to be proved, namely the objective validity of our language forms. Rather than single theories, Kant provided pairs of parallel theories; in the one case the theory of the coherence of our thinking (category) and the theory of its having content (schema); in the other, the theory of the nature of our language and the theory of the nature of intentional consciousness. But Kant knows full well that at the endpoint of each theory a connection must be made across to the endpoint of the theory parallel to it. Thus on the one hand (category and schema) the concept of substance (that which is conceived as subject only) *is* the concept of what endures through change; on the other (apperception and language) a solitary awareness of red *is* what is communicated in the utterance 'This is red'. It is not that Kant fails to *make* such connections as these. Indeed he makes them. What he is unable to do is give any reasons for making them. There is no higher theory, to which he has access, which explains how such a connection is possible. With respect to category and schema we proposed, in Chapter 3, a 'higher' theory which could embrace both aspects of concept possession without in any way compromising either aspect. Once again we need a higher theory, this time to encompass both intentional consciousness and the public language.

Consciousness as Rule-Governed

We have argued that the Transcendental Deduction cannot succeed in its final purpose. Kant is unable to show why it is that only judgment by means of the categories can yield consciousness of anything. What, we should now ask, are the implications of this failure for Kant's broader concerns about the human understanding and the nature of knowledge? It might well seem that if the argument fails then we are essentially back at the beginning of the inquiry. For consider again what it was that we expected the Deduction to show. We anticipated, in Chapter 4, an argument to the effect that there can be no such thing as an *Urerkenntnis*, an awareness of something consisting simply in that thing's being present to one's receptive consciousness, comprising nothing more than the occurrence of sense-data in a sentient being. And we expected that argument to show that there can be no awareness of anything which does not require that special unifying of data which is brought about only by the categories. Now that we know that that argument does not succeed, must we not also allow the possibility that consciousness of something should result directly from one's being sensibly affected? If this is so, then all Kant's pretensions for the special character of human understanding have foundered. A standard empiricism is once more a live option, and we have lost whatever grounds we had, or thought we had, for claiming that understanding contains something crucial within it that sensibility is in principle unable to supply.

But I think this line of reasoning is mistaken. It is wrong to suppose that Kant's argument against empiricism consists in demonstrating anything about the categories. The categories, as we saw, are brought in only late in the argument, to fill a need that has already been made out. It is the making out of that need, and not the filling of it, that constitutes Kant's argument against empiricism. We must look at this more closely. The argument against empiricism, to the effect that being sensibly affected is insufficient for being aware of anything, derives from considerations about the nature of such awareness. Every case of intentional consciousness is a situation for one; and that fact can be accounted for only by reference to a rule-governed arranging, a spontaneous synthesis of the data in consciousness. This is the nucleus of Kant's case against empiricism. It makes no reference to, does not presuppose, the categories. (Though Kant believes, mistakenly, that it points directly to them.)

But now one's suspicions might take a different form. The very fact that the path from the for-me factor to the categories is paved so neatly by the talk about synthesis, the fact that judgment-by means-of-the-categories seems so well to fill the bill of synthesis-in-one-consciousness, might make one wonder whether the whole situation was not prejudicially formulated with an eye on the categories in the first place. For what is it that makes the idea of synthesis attractive at all as an explanation of consciousness? Is it perhaps that consciousness is seen from the first as something articulated, as a spelling out of how things are, as a kind of talking to oneself? This is the suggestion that synthesis is plausible as an explanation of consciousness only because consciousness is characterized from the beginning as a kind of speaking, an internal employment of language. That is what makes it seem as if consciousness is something essentially structured, and therefore incapable of being a mere reflection of what is haphazardly given to the senses. And the implication of this suggestion will be that since we now know that Kant is unable to show that anything about language or speech is required for consciousness, we should reconsider that initial characterization of consciousness. Why should it be thought that being aware of something is anything like speaking (even to oneself)? Why, once again, shouldn't one (or an animal) simply and inarticulately be aware of red?

I think it may be true that the talk of synthesis-in-one-consciousness derives at least some of its plausibility from a forward-looking reliance on language, on judgment-by-means-of-the-categories. It is, partly, because we have, or seem to have, a relatively clear idea of what it is to put words together, in a rule-governed way, to form a communicable sentence, that we think of the operation of forming a (solitary) thought as something essentially similar. Synthesis might seem to that extent to be a *deus ex machina* in Kant's argument, conveniently brought in to make possible the transition from awareness to language.

But even to concede this is not to open the door to empiricism once more. For synthesis was introduced to solve a problem, and a problem which is not of its own making. If it is true that the data of sensibility, if they are to be anything to the one who has them, must be accompanied by the 'I think', and if that accompaniment cannot be accounted for by reference to the data, then empiricism is *already* undermined, and we need an alternative explanation of consciousness. The fact, if it is one, that Kant's alternative explanation is question-begging, or otherwise defective, does not alter this. So the fact that Kant is unable, in the Deduction, to show that the categories are involved in all consciousness does not of itself reopen the question as to whether sensibility is sufficient for consciousness. Whatever plausibility there was in the first place in the arguments for the necessity and spontaneity (non-derivability) of the for-me factor, that plausibility remains despite the failure in making the final connection to the categories. To deny Kant his final conclusion is not to deny him a significant measure of success in the argument of the Deduction.

But now our complaint against Kant will perhaps seem academic. It is easy enough, it might be thought, to understand the charge that Kant has not succeeded in showing that the categories are required for intentional consciousness so long as empiricism, or something like it, remains a viable rival candidate as an explanation of consciousness. If, however, as we have been arguing, any such possibility is independently closed off—if it is already accepted that the for-me factor cannot be accounted for by reference to sensibility, cannot be privately up to me; and if, further, the public language, judgment by means of the categories, not only succeeds in filling the bill which sensibility cannot fill, but appears to be the only candidate for that bill—then the charge that nevertheless Kant has not shown that the public language alone can do the trick is to all practical purposes empty. For what else *but* language could do the trick? We have allowed that no other candidate readily presents itself; we have no clear model for a rule-governed-state-of-affairs-for-me other than that of thoughts expressed in sentences. So we have allowed that Kant has shown that the coherent-making operations reflected in the structure of the public language, and, as far as we know, only those operations, can do what sensibility cannot do, generate the for-me factor. So what is the force of our complaint?

The complaint is not that, for all Kant has shown, sensibility might still be the source of intentional consciousness; nor is it that there are other potential rivals, apart from the public language, clamouring for that title. We may indeed be satisfied that of anything that comes to mind only the unifying acts expressed in sentences of the language meet the formal requirements adduced for anything's being a situation-for-me. What is missing in Kant is any kind of explanation as to why this should be so. *Why* is it that only the public language succeeds in providing the operations for producing the for-me factor? Why, specifically, should there not be acts productive of intentional consciousness which are *both* rule-governed *and* 'private', intelligible to me alone? It needs to be shown that these properties (rule-governedness and privacy) are incompatible with each other. Until this is shown, it will not have been demonstrated that only judgment by means of the categories can afford intentional consciousness; and so the project of the Deduction will not have succeeded.

What Kant gives us in the Deduction is a *matching* of one thing to another, of the conditions of intentional consciousness to the conditions of mutually intelligible sentences. Awareness of something requires a for-me factor, which, in turn, cannot be accounted for but by means of a spontaneous, rule-governed act; and, as it happens, we have at hand, in the very language we speak to one another, precisely such acts. This matching yields the following: to be conscious of something is to perform acts of a kind which happens to be also instantiated by the sentences of the public language. But the conclusion we need is stronger than this, namely to be conscious of something *is precisely* to perform those sentential acts; to be conscious *is* to judge by means of the categories, it is not to perform acts that are formally (and fortuitously and inexplicably) analogous to judging by means of the categories. The intended conclusion of the Deduction would seem to require that we reduce the duality here to a unity. Can this be done, without radically breaking out of the framework and the spirit of Kant's inquiry?

The connecting link, if there is one, is likely to be, or to be bound up with, the notion of rule-governedness. On the one hand we have intentional consciousness, the for-me factor, which requires for its genesis a rule-governed act. On the other hand we have sentences of the public language, the utterance of which also contains a for-me factor (it states how things are for the one who utters), and which embodies rule-governed acts. The desideratum is to show that *only* those acts embodied in the utterance of sentences can yield a situation for me. There is a gap here that needs to be filled, for why should there not be rule-governed acts, even if we cannot think of any, which are outside the public realm, and intelligible to me alone, and at the same time capable of yielding a situation-for-me? What would clearly close this gap would be a proof that rule-governedness and privacy are mutually incompatible.

Is there perhaps something about the nature of rules, or

that of following rules, that necessitates communicability or mutual intelligibility? This idea is reminiscent of
Wittgenstein, and I believe something can be made of it,
relevant to our concerns. But it needs some work.

First, to avert a possible, and rather revealing, mis-
understanding: it would be wrong to think that non-
privacy, commonality, might simply *replace* rule-
governedness; that is, that it might, other things remain-
ing the same, constitute a *sufficient* condition of the for-
me factor that rule-governedness is invoked to explain.
We noticed in the last chapter that things being thus and
so for me cannot be accounted for by reference to how
things strike me in sensibility as being. Now, given the
argument we gave there it would seem not to help
matters if we substituted for the private 'strikes-me-as-
being' a public or consensual 'strikes-us-(or most of us,
'the community') as-being'. In both cases it is mistakenly
assumed that there can be a *seeming* below the threshold
of understanding. (We will come back to this soon.) This
sort of 'publicizing' manœuvre might, however, seem
plausible *if* one supposes that what is at bottom defective
in how things privately strike me is that it is too
unreliable, too changeable, essentially too *fickle* a basis
for something as solid and stable as meaning and
understanding (the for-me factor). After all, there is no
possible restraint on how things privately strike me;
anything and everything goes. If my thought that this is
red (its being red for me[1]) is explained solely in terms of
how things seem or strike me, then that thought is
hopelessly and irremediably indeterminate. To think
that this is red is, after all, to commit oneself to thinking
of other things that are relevantly similar as also red (and
to not think of things relevantly dissimilar as red). But if
the sole basis for judgment is how things strike me then
these commitments, and the references to determinate
features of other things, unravel. There is nothing to
prevent a white swan, or for that matter the number
three, from being relevantly similar, or a ripe tomato

---

[1] NB. This isn't the same as the *thought* that it's red for me. That would be
its being red for me *for me*!

from being relevantly dissimilar. Anything and everything goes. 'One would like to say: whatever is going to seem right to me is right. And that only means that here we can't talk about "right".'[2] But thoughts are essentially right or wrong, so the basis is lacking, in how things privately strike me, for my thinking anything at all.

Now if one is struck by these sorts of considerations, by the thought that how things privately strike me is insufficiently stable to support meaning and understanding (the for-me factor), then the idea of a *consensus* might seem to remedy the situation. For if there is general agreement on how things seem, then we have something determinate and stable against which how things strike me can be measured. There will now be a criterion for its being red; there will, that is, be something I can (definitely and consistently) mean and understand by 'red'.

This explanation of understanding has the appearance of making membership in a group of communicating beings fundamental to the very existence of intentional consciousness. If I am to see anything as anything I must have direct access to how others see things. It is only *as* a member of such a community (*as* a speaker of the common language?) that I can be aware of anything. This seems to come promisingly close to what we have been looking for for so long, and complaining that Kant is unable to supply, the connection between the for-me factor and the public language.

But the explanation cannot work, and it will be instructive to see, in some detail, why it cannot. We might begin by suspecting that the explanation, assuming it to be otherwise successful, seems to explain, not the possibility of the thought that *p* (this is red), but at most the possibility of the thought that the community agrees that *p*. For it is communal agreement, on this explanation, against which I measure its striking me that *p*, and in accordance with which my thought is correct (Wittgenstein: 'right') or not. So the object of my thought, its intentional object, is apparently not *the colour* of the

[2] Wittgenstein, *Philosophical Investigations*, 2nd edn. (Oxford, 1967), §258.

thing, but rather *our agreement* as to its colour; 'this is red' means 'we all call it red'.

But now there is trouble; not just because this 'anti-realist' reduction goes counter to our intuitions, but because the matter cannot rest here. If I am to be in a position to measure how things strike me against how they strike others, I must *recognize* both. I must have the thought: 'This is how things strike me', and the thought: 'This is how they strike others'. If I do not have such thoughts, I cannot arrive at the desired thought: 'We all call it red'. But the whole purpose of the exercise (obviously not kept firmly in mind) was to explain how thought is possible. What are the conditions, we asked, for anything's being a situation for me? We do not answer this question by listing items which are themselves situations for me. I cannot arrive at my awareness from some prior position I occupy, or build it out of materials independently available to me. The question at issue, that of intentional consciousness, is simply begged here.

What has gone wrong is that general agreement, membership in the community, has entered the field at the wrong level. If agreement, or anything else, is to be a necessary condition of anything's being a thought, it may not be registered as the content of a thought I must necessarily have. It looks now as if we must somehow place this element of agreement or commonality at a deeper level, below the threshold of meaning and understanding.

What could that mean? Well, could there perhaps be a *communal sensibility*, below the plane of understanding; a primal *sensus communis*, a commonality on the ground level of being affected? This idea might seem to get support from the fact that we are, after all, members of the same animal species, having a similar sensory apparatus, etc. It will not be an objection to this proposal to urge that sensibility is necessarily below the level of commonality, since its data are essentially private, accessible only to the one affected. To suppose this is to suppose once again that sensibility is sufficient for understanding (if only private understanding), that one is aware of something (e.g. one's own sensory states) simply in virtue of being affected. But if, as we are by now taking it as established, there is no intentional consciousness at all simply in virtue of being affected, there is then no privacy barrier blocking the sharing of sensibility.

The question is, rather, what could a sharing at this level amount to, and how could it enter into the argument we are seeking? There is certainly no denying that we, human beings, and to a lesser extent many kinds of animals, have a great deal in common with respect to sensibility. On the one hand, our sensory equipment, and more generally our physiological and neurological make-up, is largely uniform. On the other hand, our natural behaviour, which expresses how we are affected, is both itself broadly similar and provoked by similar circumstances. There is every reason to believe, then, that we sense things in similar ways. Could this fact, or set of facts, constitute, or otherwise provide us with, the 'public' element which we need for the for-me factor? I do not see how it could. We are looking for something which will convert one's being 'blindly' affected into a situation for one. How could the *fact* that one is not unique in the ways and circumstances in which one is affected make any difference? Suppose I grew up and lived in total isolation from other people, would the fact of similarity still be efficacious? If so, the bearing of the similarity on my consciousness is completely obscure. So presumably not. But if the presence of others is crucial, is that because I must *recognize* their similarity to me? That will put us back in the question-begging position of the last explanation: it is precisely the possibility of such recognizings that we are attempting here to explain. Is it then that the presence of others similar to me is somehow *causally* responsible for the for-me factor? But if, as we are accepting, the reception of data is insufficient for consciousness it is quite unclear how one's being bombarded by additional data (originating from beings like oneself) could add anything.

But now it might look as if commonality, non-privacy, cannot play any role whatever in the account of intentional consciousness. In an external (causal) role, it does not do enough; in an internal role (recognition) it does too much. Either it is inefficacious, or it presupposes what it is meant to explain.

The lesson we should draw from this is that it is a mistake to look *below* the for-me factor for what makes it possible. The attempt to do so is in any case un-thought through, and does not really acknowledge (at least not consistently and deeply) the fact that inten-tional consciousness stands in need of explanation (in a way in which sensory reception does not). For these accounts invariably return to the thought that even down there things are thus and so for me. If we are persuaded that the for-me factor is not a deliverance of sensibility, we can be sure that there can be no account from below.

Does this mean that commonality, or human agree-ment, cannot enter at all into the explanation of intentional consciousness? Is there some other way than 'from below' that commonality could enter such an explanation? What we can conclude, I think, is that commonality cannot *directly* occur as a necessary condi-tion of consciousness, for then it would, it seems, have to play, from below, either a causal or an intentional role, both of which are, as we have seen ruled out. It is not ruled out, however, that commonality should enter the explanation *indirectly*, as a necessary condition or fea-ture of something else which is itself already seen to be essential (though not 'from below') to consciousness. It is not precluded, for example, that human agreement should somehow be necessary for there being any such thing as rule-governed action, where we already know that what-ever introduces the for-me factor must be rule-governed.

Let us then return to the idea of rule-governedness, in the hope that we might find something in the thought, that struck us as reminiscent of Wittgenstein, that the nature of rules, or of the following of rules, cannot be understood without reference to human agreement. Almost immediately we reach a stumbling-block, in the form of a dilemma. For what can rule-governedness amount to in the context of the claim that intentional consciousness, thought itself, is rule-governed? It would seem that if an action is rule-governed, then either (a) it is in merely 'external' accordance with the rule, subsumable under it; or (b) it is performed *as* following the rule, the rule is internal to the act. But if this is so, and if the act in question is that of transforming the allegedly blind reception of data into a situation for me, then the explanation of that act in terms of rule-governedness is doomed for the same reasons as was the previous explanation in terms of commonality. An explanation in terms of (a) is no explanation at all. It remains unaccounted for how the fact that something externally accords with a rule should yield consciousness of anything. Suppose a being, *A*, to be in a blind state of sentience; it is *ex hypothesi* unaware of anything. Suppose further that whenever *A*, or any normal member of *A*'s species, is in that state, *ceteris paribus*, it acts in a certain way, for example it utters the sound 'Aah'. So there is a rule (perhaps 'law' would be better) governing *A*'s behaviour: Whenever *A*s are in state *s*, *ceteris paribus*, they utter 'Aah'. It remains completely obscure how, if *A*'s sentient state does not itself constitute a situation for *A*, the fact that *A*'s 'response' to it is in that sense rule-governed should make any difference. If rule-governedness is plausibly to be involved in the for-me factor, it will, it seems, have to stand in closer connection to consciousness itself. The rules must, somehow, be *internal* to anything's being a situation for me.

But the alternative understanding of rule-governedness (b), seems to make the explanation of intentional consciousness circular. For if one acts not merely in accordance with what happens to be a rule, but as following the rule, *on* the rule, then one's action presumes an awareness, if only an implicit awareness, of the rule. But that means that something must be a situation for one (e.g. that this is the rule, that the rule says so-and-so) in order that one be able to engage in that act which alone is to make it possible that *anything* should be a situation for one. Once again we have failed to explain the for-me factor.

It is paradoxical, then, that intentional consciousness itself should be 'internally' rule-governed. How can something as basic as being aware of anything, as rock-bottom as having something before the mind, itself be obedient to rules? How can that which constitutes the very foundation of the understanding (Kant: the original act of the understanding) be underlain by rules? For the rules, if I act *on* them, that is on an understanding of them, must be in the understanding too. So the position at issue seems to be that awareness of anything is supported by a deeper awareness, an acceptance of rules. And it is no use protesting here: but the acceptance of the rules need only be implicit. Whatever is implicitly understood is still in the understanding, still something *for me*. (We are after all not concerned here with whether or not one can make explicit, i.e. state, the rules.)

Yet we cannot easily give up the idea that intentional consciousness is rule-governed. For whatever it is that makes the reception of data a situation for me cannot, as we have seen, be a function *of* those data, of how things primordially, below the bedrock of understanding, seem to me to be. Nor is it in any way up to me or in my hands how I arrange those data such that their presence constitutes apperception. This means that something's being a situation for me is a *determinate* affair, in no way subject to the varying data which affect me or the circumstances in which I happen to be. And it is also an *autonomous* affair, for the principle of its determinacy (its rule) cannot be imposed from outside, from 'below', the for-me factor. For if the rule were imposed from below, then again, either the for-me factor would be explained in terms of the blind reception of data (which is ruled out), or I would have grounds, in how things primordially seem, to arrange the data in such a way as to form a situation for me (which is also ruled out[3]).

---

[3] I am assuming for simplicity's sake, here and in parallel formulations, that only sensibility lies relevantly outside or below the understanding. Nothing hangs on this. If one supposed the rules to be imposed upon us by God, the results would be the same: either I am blind (deaf) to God's rule, or it is something for me. Such a rule is either incapable of explaining apperception, or it is part of the *explanandum*.

So apperception is rule-governed, and the rules are its own rules. If we leave the matter here, however, our paradox, far from being alleviated, is only intensified. We were worried just now about how something as basic as one's being aware of something can be internally rule-governed, dependent on one's acceptance of rules. We are not relieved of this worry by learning that apperception must be (autonomously) rule-governed *because* of its basicness, *because* it lies on the bedrock of the understanding. We are left with the question of how we can make sense of the idea that apperception, the original act of the understanding, should itself be internally, let alone autonomously, rule-governed.

Now I believe that our paradox here will be resolved by a correct understanding of the relationship of what we have so loosely called public agreement, or commonality, to rule-governedness. But before we consider this possibility, we should pause to note two things; first, that Kant himself, though aware of the paradox, is unable to resolve it, and secondly that his inability to do so is in the circumstances to be expected.

The paradox, in its broadest form, is that understanding as such should be internally rule-governed, that for anything to be anything for one is for it to defer to rules. The paradoxicality of this situation can be seen from the fact that it invites an unstoppable regress. If P is to be anything for me, then it involves my acceptance of rule R. If R is to be accepted by me, it must itself be something for me, and as such will involve the further acceptance of Rule R_1, which, in turn . . . and so on *ad infinitum*. Now it would seem to be a way out of this regress if one could give an interpretation of 'R is accepted by me' which does not immediately yield 'R is something for me'. And this is in fact the route chosen by Kant. The bottom line where anything is anything for me is the act of synthesis in one consciousness, apperception. Below that act nothing is anything for me. But the act itself is attentive to rules (the categories). So there must be a level of the understanding, inhabited by these rules, that is deeper than the for-me factor—a level where it can truly be said that an item is *in* the understanding while not as such, or not yet, being anything for me. Kant clearly means to have it both ways.

But this is an untenable position. It is crucial, first, that the rules be located in the understanding, and not elsewhere, for example in sensibility, or left unlocated. For apperception, the basic act of understanding, is *spontaneous*, not in any way derived from or made to fit anything else; so the rules to which it attends must be, as it were, wherever apperception itself is, not in some other underlying place. The for-me factor does not and cannot take anything outside itself into account—for if it did it would presuppose another for-me factor. Understanding can pay no attention to what is not already in it. So it is important that the categories not only make possible the understanding, but that they have their home there. Now the difficulty in all this is not that Kant has made no room for something's being in the understanding while not as such being anything for one, but that no room for such a possibility can be made. The force of the claim that the categories are in the understanding, and not elsewhere, is quite lost if to be in the understanding is allowed to be compatible with not being anything for me. For the rationale of saying that the categories, or whatever are the rules of apperception, cannot derive from elsewhere, for example from sensibility, is that in sensibility, or anywhere else outside apperception itself, nothing is anything for me. But that means that if the categories are located on an alleged level of the understanding below the for-me factor, no advantage is gained over locating them in sensibility. In both cases they are to be found on a level on which we are, as yet, blind. Any features existing on this level cannot therefore be taken by us into account in our awareness of anything.

So Kant is driven by the paradoxical nature of the autonomy of apperception to postulate something which cannot exist, a level of the understanding below apperception, and thus to betray his own conviction that understanding, by contrast with sensibility, is from beginning to end a matter of how things are for one. (See B133 n., 'this faculty of apperception is the understanding itself'.) This betrayal is doubtless aided and abetted by the uncritically accepted 'faculty psychology', in particular by the picture of the understanding as an intellectual machine, a motor which even when not actually functioning has capacities and conditions which belong to its nature. Such a picture is of course by no means useless in all circumstances, but it is certainly useless here, where we are proceeding *from* the claim that apperception, while standing in need of an explanation, cannot be explained from any position outside, or 'below', itself. The argument from blindness applies, in the end, as devastatingly to Kant's own account of consciousness as it does to his predecessors' accounts. If neither sensibility (Locke), nor innate capacities or dispositions (Leibniz) can yield the for-me factor, nor can Kant's categories. *All* these suffer from having their being below the level of apperception itself.

But observe, now, the position we have reached. In attempting to see whether Kant's failure to connect intentional consciousness with the public language can be rectified (by pursuing the idea of rule-governed action) we have stumbled upon what appears to be another, perhaps deeper, failure on Kant's part. He is unable, we have now claimed, ultimately to distinguish his own account of consciousness from that of his predecessors. Like them, he succumbs to what is in fact just another explanation 'from below', the futility of which, in general, he has so persistently insisted upon.

I do not think, however, that we are dealing here with something merely accidental. I believe that given the one failure the other is inevitable, and further that both of these hang together with a third (Chapter 2), the failure to connect category with schema. If Kant were in a position to give an explanation of intentional consciousness which is not 'from below', he would also be in a position to connect consciousness with the public language and category with schema. Conversely, if he could have connected these items with one another he would have been able to avoid an explanation from below.

We will come back to this theme soon. But first we should ask what an explanation of intentional consciousness that is not 'from below' could consist in. And this will mean, in the context of our discussion, returning to our paradox that apperception itself should be (internally) rule-governed. How can we make sense of the idea that to be aware of something at all is to act on rules? We need both to avoid an infinite regress of situations-for-me and to resist Kant's desperate strategy of building the rules into a mechanism below the for-me factor. What we will need to show is that apperception involves a genuine *acceptance* or *recognition* of the rules without thereby being *grounded in* such an acceptance or recognition. The rules, in other words, must somehow be capable of being something for me and at the same time on a plane with, and not prior to, the act that is to introduce the for-me factor. This is indeed a tall order to fill. In Kant's terms, it will mean that the possibility of apperception requires that there be categories in the understanding, while what it is for there to be categories in the understanding is nothing at all apart from the fact that we perform acts of apperception. But now an additional worry presents itself. For even if we can make sense of there being categories in the understanding (of our accepting rules) on this account, won't it be the case that reference to categories, or rules, will lose all of its explanatory force? Yet the very point of this enterprise was to explain how apperception, and thereby consciousness of anything, is possible. We must return to this worry too. But first, can we make sense of awareness as rule-following?

If we are to see the act that makes awareness of something possible (i.e. the act that introduces the for-me factor) as a rule-following act, then we must see it as somehow *revealing* an awareness of rules without its being the case that such action *presupposes* a (prior) awareness of rules. Now I think this tells us something very important about the nature of the act in question.

What is the act that brings about the for-me factor? Whatever else it might be, it ought surely to be an act of thinking that *p*, of composing a thought (*p*) in one's mind, of representing things to oneself as being *p*. That act, if it is to be rule-following, must, we now know, be such that we can see it as revealing or implying an awareness (*q*) of rules, without its therefore being the case that the thought that *p* contains the further thought that *q* (that these are the rules). But that means that the act in question cannot, simply and finally, be an act of (pure) thinking. If it were, then anything implied or revealed in the act would have to be contained in the thought. If, to bring this point into sharper focus, the act (of thinking) is visible only from the inside, if the only access to it is in first-person terms, as composing a situation for me, and if that act is to involve the awareness of rules, then that awareness would itself have to be in first-person terms. For there is no room, within apperception conceived in this exclusively self-reflexive way, for anything that is not explicitly present to it. The rules would then present themselves as thus and so for me, and would thus be objects of awareness, and there would be no avoiding the infinite regress of successive awarenesses. What this means, I think, is that if intentional consciousness is, in the last analysis, nothing beyond what it is *for* the one whose consciousness it is, if the only real access to it is from the inside, from a first-person perspective, then we cannot make sense of the idea that awareness involves the acceptance of rules. Awareness conceived on this model cannot fail to be completely illuminated from within—or there is utter darkness, and so no awareness at all. If, then we are to make sense of the idea that awareness involves the acceptance of rules, we must somehow break out of our Cartesian shell and come to see awareness from a larger perspective; the fundamentality of the first-person point of view must give way to something else.

Now this conclusion is in fact completely in line with a central feature of Kant's own position. For Descartes, the 'I think', the ego-reflexive perspective, is the ultimate core of consciousness. For Kant it is not. The 'I think' (the analytic unity of consciousness) is itself underlain by synthesis, by an act which involves rules which are not themselves accompanied by the 'I think'. The difficulty with Kant, as we saw, is not that he represents the rules for awareness as objects of awareness, thus subjecting himself to an infinite regress of awarenesses, but the contrary difficulty—that he permits the rules to slip below the threshold of awareness altogether, and thus renders himself incapable of showing how awareness of anything involves the *acceptance* of rules. Kant rightly means to reject the Cartesian picture of human consciousness, what we are calling the exclusively ego-reflexive point of view. The 'I think' is not ultimate, it itself stands in need of deeper explanation. But he has failed to provide a viable alternative picture, and so he has failed to show how it is possible that something that is not itself accompanied by the 'I think' should nevertheless belong to the *understanding*, be an integral part of what it is to be conscious of something.

So we are looking for nothing less than the ultimate ground of intentional consciousness. We know that this ground, whatever else it might be, is an act that we perform, a spontaneous, underived, rule-following act. We also know that it cannot, at bottom, be an act *of* apperception pure-and-simple, as it is in Descartes; for apperception itself needs grounding. And we have now come upon a further condition that this grounding act must satisfy: it must in principle be accessible from more than the single, first-person point of view. It must have an outside as well as an inside, for otherwise it cannot sensibly be seen as a rule-following act. And this in turn suggests something else, namely that what we are seeking is not so much a *ground* for consciousness— something on which it rests, which supports it from beneath—as a *body* for it, a context, something for it to inhabit, which incorporates it. For what we need is an action that is on a plane with, not lying below, apperception, and that, at the same time, affords a perspective other than the first-person one. We need, as a minimum, an act that involves or includes apperception but which apperception does not exhaust.

Now, there is nothing that satisfies these conditions other than a certain class of human actions; those actions, namely, which *express* our awareness that so-and-so, and which thus *both* involve apperception *and* are visible from the outside. These are (or better: include) the acts that Kant has been aiming at all along, assertoric speech acts, acts of judging in the public language. But whereas Kant was unable, as we saw, to give any reason for making the transition from rule-governed synthesis to publicly accessible judgment, we have given at least the beginnings of such a reason. We have succeeded, I hope, in showing that awareness cannot be regarded as rule-following unless it is more broadly conceived than as a mere first-person perspective. What we have yet to do is indicate just how the addition of a further perspective, or further perspectives, *does* enable us to see awareness as rule-following.

What we have already succeeded in showing in fact goes quite a long way. Our complaint against Kant, in the Deduction, was that he is unable to explain why it is that only what is mutually intelligible can satisfy the requirements of apperception, that is generate a rule-governed situation for one. Why we asked, should there not be acts productive of consciousness(-of-objects) which are *both* rule-governed *and* private, intelligible to me alone? We now have an answer to this question. For we have argued that rule-governedness and privacy are indeed incompatible. We have argued this, not in general (as Wittgenstein does, see below), but with respect only to apperception itself, the 'original act of the understanding'. If awareness itself is to be regarded as rule-following, then there must be access to it from outside itself. For if there is not—to spell this out once more—if the very being of awareness is exhausted in what is present from a first-person point of view, then the only way in which awareness could involve the acceptance of rules would be if the rules too constituted an actual situation for one, and so an infinite regress of situations for one would be launched. (And it is a vicious regress, for it reduces the claim that the acceptance of rules is a necessary condition for anything's being a situation for one to triviality: *p* is a necessary condition of *p*.) But that there must be access to awareness from outside means nothing less than that the content of the awareness cannot be intelligible only to the one whose awareness it is, but must be communicable. So we have found a reason for making the transition from the rule-governedness of consciousness to its communicability.

But just what role does this non-privacy, communicability, of awareness play in the question of its rule-governedness? We know now that the Cartesian picture of awareness as nothing over and above a first-person perspective does not leave room for its being rule-governed, and that therefore if awareness is rule-governed it must be accessible from outside, and thus, being what it is, communicable. But this does not tell us *how* communicability enters into the business of rule-governedness. How, in what way, can the fact that my thought that this is red is intelligible to another person make it possible that in thinking it to be red I am following rules?

Now, the requirement that we have uncovered for the rule-governedness of awareness is in fact more complicated than simply that awareness be communicable or accessible from outside the first-person perspective. What we need as an embodiment of awareness is not merely something which has an outside as well as an inside, but rather something whose outside can also, but need not, be seen from the inside. We need something which has features of which it is essential that they are capable of being something for me but do not consist in being something for me.[4] And we need this last characteristic (that there be features capable of being, but not consisting of being, something for me) as a necessary condition of awareness itself, not, for example, as some additional item that presupposes my awareness. All this we need in our 'embodiment' of awareness, in the act

[4] It must be *possible* for the 'I think' to accompany all my representations.

that is to introduce the for-me factor, *if* we are to make sense of the peculiar way in which the rules governing awareness play their role, as implicit in one's thinking without being what one thinks, as present in the understanding without thereby being objects of the understanding.

So it seems that if we are to locate the species of act that is responsible for consciousness of objects, we must find, in the realm of human action that is expressive of thought, something that satisfies this complex requirement. We should note, first, that an isolated case of assertion, of saying that so-and-so ('It's red'), torn from all context of utterance, will not be enough. For though it has not only an outside as well as an inside, but one that can be seen from inside (I can attend to what I say), there seems to be no way of seeing that that outside, capable of being seen from within, is crucial to there being an inside in the first place. The fact that you hear me say it's red, or that I can hear myself say it, seems clearly posterior to my awareness, my thinking, that it's red, hardly a condition of it. Indeed, any concentration on the isolated utterance appears to entrench the Cartesian picture more deeply, rather than to weaken its hold. For what, it is plausible to ask, is it to *say* it's red than to give voice to one's thought, to find appropriate vocables (Locke) for the already present ideas?

We clearly need something that is somehow *larger* than an episode of speaking. But, in particular, we need something that displays that it has in itself room for what is *implicit* in one's thinking. The Cartesian picture, the idea of awareness or thinking as exhaustively the first-person perspective, can make no sense, after all, of the idea of something's being implicitly, or latently, contained in one's thinking, as being present in one's thought but not explicitly or expressly so. For to be present at all, on this picture, is to be present *to me, here and now*; in the realm of cogitare everything is directly open to me, if it exists at all. Kant, on the other hand, needs and wants to allow room for the implicit in consciousness, for the categories must be precisely that, implicit in consciousness. So Kant must break with the Cartesian picture. Yet his placing of the categories below the level of explicit presence to consciousness does not succeed in explaining what it is meant to explain, how the categories function *in* our awareness of anything, as opposed to being, like being sensibly affected, an external pre-condition of awareness. So Kant has, in the end, not really broken with the Cartesian picture; he has not made room for the position he needs, between something's being expressly present to me on the one hand, and my being blind to it on the other.

But now a tension has developed in our argument. On the one hand we seem to want to say that acts of assertion or judgment in the public language, *are* the acts we have been looking for all along, the spontaneous, rule-following acts required for the for-me factor. On the other hand we are now apparently claiming that such (isolated) acts are somehow insufficient for what is needed. There are two interrelated questions here, which we have perhaps allowed to drift into one another in the last few pages, but which now need to be carefully disentangled. The first question concerns the identity of the act that is required for consciousness of anything. It is the question of what sort of action qualifies as spontaneous and rule-following. And our answer, in agreement with Kant, is: judgment in the public language. (But we, unlike Kant, have been able to find a reason for making this identification, a reason, that is, for insisting that the act in question be a mutually intelligible one.) The other question is a deeper one. It is the question of what makes it possible that these acts of judgment (e.g. calling something red) should qualify as spontaneous and rule-governed. For they do not display these characteristics on their surface. Indeed, as we have noted, it seems natural to see an act of saying something, if we consider it in isolation, as the outward communicable sign of the real apperception, that is, as derived from a private thought. Further, and connectedly, though we have now given *a* reason for identifying judgment in the public language as the rule-following act that is to introduce the for-me factor, our doing so has not yet relieved the paradoxicality of the claim that awareness is rule-governed. *How* can judgment in the public language be *both* the basic underived act of consciousness *and* rule-accepting? We need to go beyond the identification of the act and to show how it is that acts of judgment involve the implicit acceptance of rules. We must see such acts as displaying a knowledge of the rules without thereby seeing them as being underlain by knowledge of the rules. What then is it to know the rules, where such knowledge is so intimately bound up with (and does not come from below) the acts that display it?

A solution to this problem, and I think the only satisfactory one, is to see the knowledge thus displayed as essentially and irreducibly *practical*. This would be to regard knowledge of the rules not as something which, though here and there manifested in action, has its real being elsewhere, but as something which is essentially bound up with the manifestation itself. Such knowledge must be seen to lie in or around the actions that display it, not behind them. But how? How are we to see acceptance of rules in or around such actions as judging something to be, say red, or a slab, or a cube? This is a question that Wittgenstein asks. And he answers as follows. We cannot make sense of such actions as being rule-accepting, as displaying knowledge of the rules, if we look upon them as the outward manifestation of something lying hidden behind them. We can make sense of such actions as rule-accepting if (and indeed only if) we see them as instantiations of a skill, as exemplifications of the mastery of a practice or technique.

In order to see this, we need to discuss the nature of rule-following in an unrestricted way, without confining ourselves, as we have been, to the act of apperception itself—the action the performance of which first introduces the for-me factor.

Wittgenstein has a general argument to the effect that to know rules, such that one can act on them, is to be at home with, to have mastered, to be in practical command of, a system, a technique, a practice, a web of human actions in which there are moves to be made and roles to be taken. A favourite illustration of Wittgenstein's, though one liable to mislead, is that of a rule-governed game such as chess. One's ability to play chess, to act on the rules (on one's understanding of the rules) of the game is fundamentally an irreducibly and homogeneously practical matter. It is not to be thought of in ultimately dualistic terms, as, on the one hand, a species of bodily behaviour, made possible by (arising from), on the other hand, an intellectual state or process, the understanding of the rules. If the understanding of the rules is thought of as something ontologically distinct from the actions that arise from or embody that understanding, then there will be an unbridgeable gulf between the alleged understanding and the actions, and we will be prevented from seeing how one can act on an understanding of rules at all.

To bring out the issues here we will consider what might be regarded as an intuitively natural account of what it is to follow or act on rules. Suppose that someone customarily (in the way chess players do) moves his bishop only on the diagonal, corrects mistakes on the part of learners, etc.—thereby manifesting his knowledge of the rule. What, let us ask, does his knowing or understanding of the rule actually consist in? We do not, of course, want to *equate* the knowing of the rule with the bodily movement of the bishop along the diagonal; for the movement can occur without the knowing, and the knowing be present though no movement is made. The knowing, we will want to say, is something in the mind that *explains* the bodily movement.[5] It is the player's *information* that the bishop moves (may move, must move) only on the diagonal. But what is it to possess that information, such that one acts on it as one does when playing chess? It is, of course, to be aware that this is how the piece moves. And what is that? One might think, first, that it is to *have the thought* that this is how it moves. But no such thought need

----

[5] Wittgenstein, *Investigations*, e.g. §146.

actually occur—and might even be suspect in an accomplished player. And now it will look as if what had at first to be consciously borne in mind can, with practice, be taken over by unconscious processes. Whereas the beginner had to keep the rule explicitly before his consciousness, the practised player needs no longer to attend to it, for it will continue to exert its influence on his actions from below the level of consciousness. Just what that state, below the level of consciousness might be is, one might then suppose, a question for neurophysiology, or whatever might be the appropriate branch of cognitive science. But now it seems that we are on familiar ground, with another variant of the ill-fated explanation from below. If knowledge of the rule is assigned a location below the level of consciousness, then it is impossible to see how one can act *on* such knowledge. (Which is not to deny that the brains of practised chess players might, unlike those of all other people, be in a certain state precisely with reference to the ability of those players to execute such moves.)

But the objection to explanations from below does not seem as convincing in the present case as it did when we considered such explanations in a general way before. For it is a crucial part of the account now before us that the rules of chess were *once* on the forefront of the practised player's consciousness. They are not, as Kant's categories unfortunately seem to be, located from the beginning below the level of apperception. So this account of what it is to act on rules is not really or finally an explanation from below at all. The player's knowledge of the rules is not something originally hidden from his view—though it is something which by natural processes will, with habituation and practice, recede to a position beneath the level of his consciousness.

The present account does not take *implicit* knowledge of rules to be fundamental; rather it takes it to be a natural successor to *explicit* knowledge of rules. The idea, broadly, is this. To act in accordance with a rule is, basically (originally), to behave in a certain way, where that behaviour is directed by a conscious thought or awareness that this is how one is to behave. With practice in the relevant behaviour, the thought or awareness will normally sink below the conscious level. (But only just below it!—and ready to rise to the surface once more if called upon. We would expect the practised player to *cite* the rule if, for example, asked by someone who knows nothing of the game why he moved the bishop on the diagonal.)

Now, our earlier objection to placing the rules within the content of consciousness, regarding them as objects of consciousness, does not apply here. For we were talking there only of rules governing intentional consciousness, the for-me factor, itself. And one cannot, we saw, without engendering an infinite regress, regard the rules necessary for one's being aware of anything as themselves items of which one is aware. But now we are considering rule-following without this restriction; and nothing we argued earlier, it seems, makes it impossible that rule-following actions *other* than the act of apperception itself should be seen in the way here contemplated—as directed, from within, by what is basically and originally a conscious awareness of the rule.

But it is far from clear that this is a tolerable situation. For on the one hand we are accepting the idea that the rules that govern the act of apperception, the act that introduces the for-me factor, are essentially implicit in consciousness, where their being implicit there is something quite basic and underived. And on the other hand, we are being asked to accept the idea that for other (presumably all other?) rule-governed actions, the implicitness of the rules in our consciousness in performing these acts is something essentially derivative; in these other cases it is essential that the rules are originally present in the mind explicitly, as objects of consciousness.

Now, there are doubtless differences among rules, and among kinds of rules, and different ways in which rules might be followed. But it would be disconcerting if what it is to act on a rule were ultimately and irreducibly a matter of two radically different kinds of things. In the one case (in line with what we have been saying about the chess example) one follows a rule when, and only when, one's behaviour is grounded in, stems from, something quite different from behaviour, namely an intellectual act of recognition. In the other case (to which we have been led in our Kantian investigation) there is no such grounding act at all—the behaviour itself is somehow ultimate. We surely cannot let the matter rest here. If the grounding act is in the one case necessary for the behaviour to be rule-following, how can it be simply missing in the other case and the behaviour there still be rule-following? Alternatively, if we can make sense of behaviour as rule-following in that other case in the absence of a grounding act of intellect, why should such an act be necessary anywhere? How, in short, can there be two radically divergent sets of conditions for the application of what is surely a single concept—that of acting on (the understanding of) rules? One would hope for some ultimate unity here.

Now there would seem to be only two possible ways of arriving at such unity:

Either (a) one insists upon and generalizes what we have called the 'natural' account of what it is to act on a rule. A rule-following action would thus in every case ultimately be underlain by (grounded in, directed by) a conscious awareness of the rules. This manœuvre has the immediate consequence of bringing our Kantian investigation to a halt: implicit rule-consciousness always has explicit rule-consciousness in its history, and so the 'original' act of the understanding, awareness itself, could not be a rule-following act at all. One resolves the Kantian paradox by showing the desired state of affairs to be contradictory.

Or (b) one takes the opposite course, and generalizes the findings, as arrived at so far, of our Kantian investigation. One's awareness of the rules on which one acts is, on this view *always* ultimately an *implicit* matter. But how, one might ask, could one plausibly hold such a view? Isn't explicit rule-consciousness a plain and basic *fact*?—well, it might be arguable that where rules are explicitly present to consciousness, the possibility of their being so is *itself* underlain by one's capacity to act on an implicit understanding of rules. We must examine this line of argument, which is Wittgenstein's, with attention, if we are to reach our Kantian goal and come to understand how it is possible that awareness itself should be rule-governed. For what prevents us from understanding how this is possible is precisely that we are captivated by the idea of explicit rule-consciousness as a basic phenomenon, as something complete unto itself, that underlies, and explains, rule-following behaviour.

We need to look more closely at explicit rule-consciousness. Take a case that is simpler than the rules of chess. When we see a large pointing sign (e.g.→) on the wall, say at an airport, we understand it to mean that this, the direction indicated, is the way to go (given certain standard conditions, objectives, desires, etc.).[6] And, other things being equal and normal (we have just come off the plane) this will be the way we in fact go. Now let us ask, as Wittgenstein does, what this sign, which I see, has to do with my actions. 'What sort of connection is there here?'[7] Well, one wants to say, my acting as I do on seeing the sign is of course not directly caused by my seeing the sign—as my falling is caused by my being pushed—but, rather, it is *mediated* by an understanding, a grasp, of what the signs means. I see the sign and understand that this is the direction in which to go; and that is why I go in that direction. Again, this understanding might be, as we say, 'automatic', facilitated by long habituation: I look up, see the sign and without a thought proceed in the direction indicated. But suppose it is not (yet) automatic. Suppose, for whatever reason—perhaps because, as a visitor from abroad, I am not accustomed to these signs—I have to think of the

---

[6] For simplicity's sake I am imagining the pointing arrow to be unaccompanied by any words: it simply points the way to go, when e.g. leaving the plane or entering the subway. Not, of course, that there is no other way to go; there are, e.g. doors leading off the corridor. Ideally there would be arrows in the vicinity of such doors indicating, indirectly, that the way to go is not through them. I think nothing is lost by such simplification.

[7] Wittgenstein, *Investigations*, §198.

rule, actually bring it to consciousness. I stand there blank, or perplexed, facing the sign, and then it suddenly comes to me: of course, TURN RIGHT; and I proceed to the right. This sort of case will seem to be a paradigm of rule-consciousness, in a way in which the automatic case will not—not because such cases occur more commonly than the automatic cases, which they do not, but because (or so it appears) it is only with reference to such explicit cases that we can see the automatic, or implicit, ones as rule-following at all. The behaviour (turning right) can be seen as manifesting an awareness of the rule only because, in each of us, such behaviour was first made possible by our actually holding the rule in consciousness. In this explicit case it seems that we can see the very essence of what it is to act on a rule: the rule is plainly there for me (of course, TURN RIGHT), and I immediately act accordingly, turning right.

Now the question we need to ask is not whether such explicit rule-consciousness is *necessary* for one's action to be rule-following. We have already allowed that it is not (though we are imagining, for the time being, that the non-explicit cases are to be explained with reference to the explicit ones). Our question is whether the characterization we have given is *sufficient* for the action to be rule-following. But we need to be careful here. Of course, if the rule consciously occurs to one and one then acts on it, *that* will be sufficient for one's following the rule. The question is, however, whether one's acting on the rule is sufficiently provided for by its being granted that the rule consciously occurs to one and that one then acts accordingly. The occurring of the rule in the mind of the foreign visitor, when he saw the sign, was to constitute his understanding of the sign, his grasp of what it meant. It was this mental occurrence that was to mediate his seeing the sign and his turning right, and thereby make that action what it would not otherwise be, one of acting on what the sign told him, of following a rule. But it is clear that the occurring of 'turn right' in the visitor's consciousness will not be sufficient to constitute his understanding of the sign *unless it is itself understood by him.* But it need not be. *That* the phrase occurs in one's consciousness does not entail that one understands it. It might be, for example that seeing the sign awakens in the foreign visitor an association, derived perhaps from his English phrasebook, and the words 'turn right' pop into his mind. He, understanding neither sign nor phrase, nevertheless proceeds to the right, together with everyone else. Nor need the phrase that occurs to him be foreign to him for him to fail to grasp it correctly. It may be that he associates the sign with the words 'turn right' in his own language, but fails to take either the sign or the words to be addressed to him; nevertheless, he turns right, with the rest of the crowd. (Or—the variations here are endless—he takes it as addressed to him, but as some sort of report of what some people sometimes do. Or he might take it as addressed to him, and even as an instruction to him, to the effect that he is to meditate on the manœuvre of the right turn; which he does and nevertheless, independently of this, follows the crowd.)

The question we need to ask is: In virtue of what is something that occurs in the mind—for example the formula 'turn right'—a case of understanding *that this is what one is to do*—turn right? What sort of thing do we have to add to the occurring of the formula to make it a case of knowing what to do when the formula occurs to one? The mere explicit presence of the formula in one's consciousness is not, we have seen, enough. And nothing that we might add, or find, on the level on which the formula occurs will help. No further element in consciousness alongside the formula will do what is needed, convert the mere ('blind') occurrence of the formula into knowledge of what to do. For whatever we might find there—and what might be a candidate: additional instructions: turn right: this is what I am to do now, or visions of oneself and others moving to the right perhaps under compulsion, or feelings of being drawn to the right?—there will still be the question of understanding, of knowing how to act on, *it*.

We were looking for something in consciousness to

mediate, to connect, the seeing of the sign (→) and the outward behaviour, turning right. We needed such a medium, we thought, if we were to be able to see that behaviour as one of going by, or acting on, the sign. But now it is clear that whatever we find in consciousness stands in need of just such mediation itself; it too, as much as the sign in the first place, needs to be provided with a connection to the behaviour that is to flow from it, if it *is* to flow from it. It should be clear now that in looking for such a medium we have been looking for something that cannot exist. It would have to be something which, while having its own total being in consciousness, and whose essence is therefore quite distinct from behaviour, is nevertheless essentially, by its own nature, connected with behaviour. For if it is not connected to behaviour by its own nature, then it will need a further something to afford the connection; and if it does not have its total being in consciousness, then it is not what it was designed to be, the alleged *Urphänomen* of explicit rule-consciousness.

But now it might look as if we are denying that there can be any such thing at all as rule-consciousness, as knowing what to do when confronted with the sign, or with anything else. For it seems that we are denying that anything in the mind, conscious or unconscious, can mediate between the item before me, whatever it is, and the action that it calls for. We argued earlier that nothing below the level of consciousness can do the job—I cannot act on an understanding of what to do if what I am to do is not, and never was, present to my consciousness. And now we seem to have claimed that nothing in my consciousness can do the job either. For if it is something in my consciousness then it is another item confronting me about which the question of my knowing how to act given the presence of that item will once again arise. So *knowing how to act* must itself lie hidden beneath the surface of consciousness—from which subterranean regions we have however already banished it. It seems, then, that there is nowhere in the mind, in the psychological make-up, for rule-consciousness to exist. We must either face the sceptical conclusion that there is really no such thing; or we must accept some sort of reductionist (perhaps behaviouristic) account of what it is to act on a rule, an account which does not include among its elements a grasp or understanding of the rule as that which connects the item confronted and the action which, as we say, accords with it. (This, though the emphasis is different, is essentially the position that Saul Kripke attributes to Wittgenstein.)[8]

But all this is highly paradoxical. For surely there is such a phenomenon as following a rule—as, for example following, or going by, the sign →. And when one does follow that sign it is precisely one's understanding of what that sign means, one's consciousness of what it is telling one to do, that connects the sign to one's turning right. Any other connection[9] would be incompatible with one's following the sign.

Now there is in fact nothing in our argument that denies that there is a connection between the sign → and one's turning right, when one follows the sign. Nor does anything in the argument deny that that connection *is* one's understanding, or consciousness, of what the sign is telling one to do. What is being denied is that that understanding or consciousness can be identified with any item that occurs in one's consciousness—that is, that there is any item in one's consciousness whose mere presence is sufficient for one's knowing what to do on seeing the sign. To deny that one's knowing what to do on seeing the sign is a middle thing straddling the gap between the seeing of the sign and the doing (and, as an occurrent phenomenon, homogeneous with both) is not to deny that there is such a thing as knowing what to do on seeing the sign.

The mistake here, as we anticipated earlier, is that of taking what we have called explicit rule-consciousness to be the basic phenomenon at issue. We take, as giving the essence of what it is to know the rule, having before

---

[8] Saul Kripke, *Wittgenstein on Rules and Private Language* (Blackwell, 1981).
[9] e.g. if seeing the sign arouses in me an inclination to turn right, which I then act on, then I am not following a rule, I am following my appetite.

the mind what Wittgenstein calls an 'interpretation' of the rule, a reformulation of what one is being told to do. But now we know that whatever the reformulation in the mind (e.g. 'turn right') there is still the question of knowing what *it* is telling one to do. Such an interpretation or reformulation is only of use to someone who already knows what to do with it. (Interpretations and reformulations can of course be useful and are sometimes necessary; where for example the sign → is unfamiliar to one. Here, remembering the phrase-book, or being told that it means 'turn right' would be very much to the point.)

What this shows is not that there is no such thing as understanding what one is supposed to do on seeing the sign, but that such understanding is not what we thought it to be, a matter of interpreting, of giving oneself or being given the meaning of the sign. Explicit rule-conscious-ness does not, then, constitute one's knowing the rule, it presupposes it. So the conclusion of our general inquiry, so far, into the nature of rule-following is the same as that of our Kantian investigation: in neither case, and so in no case, can one's acceptance or awareness of a rule be construed as the content of one's consciousness. And, though there are differences, the main reason why one's awareness of a rule cannot be construed in this way is the same in the general case as in the Kantian one. If one's being aware of the rule is a matter of having it before the mind then it (the rule before the mind) will constitute just another item for the understanding of which the awareness of just such a rule is invoked. So awareness of rules must always, at bottom, be an *implicit* matter.

How are we to spell out the nature of this implicit awareness that we have found to be fundamental? Well, how are we to bring out the difference between ourselves when we go by the sign and the foreign visitor who does not understand the sign? The difference seems obvious, and very simple: we are familiar with the sign, used to it, accustomed to it; he is not. Nothing else distinguishes us from him. If he were accustomed to the sign as we are accustomed to it, he would be one of us. But what does this familiarity, this being accustomed to the sign amount to? It is not enough that we are used to *seeing* the sign and that he is not. For he might be, and it could still mean nothing to him. But now, if the sign means something to us and not to the foreign visitor, and that fact is to be a function of its being familiar to us and not to him, then it looks as if our familiarity with the sign amounts to this: for us, but not for him, the sign is associated, by long habit, with a certain action, that of turning right; and so, with us, seeing the sign brings that action (vividly) to mind, we have the thought 'turn right'. For the foreign visitor that action is not brought to mind, he has no such thought, and so he does not understand the sign. But this is where we were before. No such thing needs to be brought to mind in our case, though we understand the sign; and just such a thing might occur in his mind, though he does not understand it. And in any case whatever might occur in one's mind on seeing the sign, it would itself have to be understood by one, and thus in turn, familiar to one. If familiarity, custom, is to be of help to us in our quest for the nature of rule-conscious-ness we must not look upon it as a mere and external means to an alleged real and internal end, an explicit thought in the mind.

What is crucial is not that, as a result of our customary behaviour with the sign, seeing the sign gives us ideas, but simply, and finally, our customary behaviour with the sign. We are used to *reacting* to it in a certain way, we have the practice of turning right when we see it (given the appropriate objectives and desires, etc.). Our having this practice, our being accustomed to behaving in this way in these circumstances is itself the *Urphänomen*, the basic phenomenon at issue. It is this, and this alone, that constitutes our awareness of the rule, our knowing what to do on seeing the sign. We must resist the temptation to see the practice as the outcome of something that lies behind it in the understanding, as if a prior awareness or recognition of what the sign means could account for how we customarily treat it. We see now that no candidate for such an underlying awareness can amount to anything more than an interpretation, an inner substitute for the sign, and cannot escape being the focus of the same questions and difficulties that beset the sign in the first place. If merely seeing the sign is insufficient to explain one's behaviour, then so also is merely seeing, or hearing, 'turn right', or anything else, in one's mind. If, on the other hand, hearing 'turn right' in one's mind *in the right way* is sufficient (as it is), then so also is seeing the sign in the first place *in the right way*. And here seeing it in the right way does not mean aligning it with something else (e.g. something internal) that one sees—for then the connection to one's actions would still need to be made—but *treating* it in a certain way, namely as the familiar thing it is, a signpost.

But now it might seem that the pendulum has swung too far in the other direction. If the very essence of our understanding the sign → (our knowing the rule) is nothing but our possession of the practice, the way we customarily react to the sign, then indeed there will be no difficulty (of the kind we have been considering) about *connecting* the phenomenon of understanding with the actual behaviour that accords with it, there will be no problematic gap here still waiting to be filled. But—and for the very reason that that gap is firmly closed—it might look as if this account suffers from the same defect as the various 'explanations from below' we considered earlier: consciousness appears to be left out of the picture. How, one might ask, can one's action (say, of turning right) be properly seen to be performed *on one's understanding* of the rule, as opposed to being merely in external accordance with the rule, *if* one's understanding of the rule consists of nothing that is present to the mind, but is simply a matter of how one (customarily) behaves? Surely, the rule (or sign) must somehow constitute a situation *for* one, if one is to *follow* it.

Now we are indeed claiming that one's understanding of the sign does not consist of anything that is present to the mind (for whatever is present to the mind itself needs to be understood). What still needs to be made fully clear is that this does not mean that consciousness—and indeed a first-person perspective—is being left out of the picture. We should remind ourselves here of what has been our main theoretical requirement for some time. We argued earlier that if the spirit of Kant's enterprise is to be borne out and consciousness of objects is to be seen as rule-following, then the act which embodies that consciousness must be seen to *display* our knowledge of the rules without being *underlain* by that knowledge. This is still our main requirement (though we have now shown that it covers *all* rule-following actions, since rule-consciousness is always ultimately implicit in the actions that display it). To fulfil this requirement, with our present example, would be to find *in* our customary behaviour with respect to the directional sign the *expression* of our consciousness (of what it means, that we are to turn right)—where that expression is not to be construed as the outward and publicly visible clothing of something inward and visible only to oneself. But it seems as if the only alternative to seeing the behaviour as the outward clothing of the inward phenomenon is to see it as brute, or mechanical, movement, as something thoroughgoingly physical and third-personal.

What does one's awareness of what the sign means—that one is to turn right—consist in, if not in something actually present to one's consciousness (an occurrent thought)? Here, as Wittgenstein would say, we need only describe what we all know, what is in plain view. Our understanding of the sign consists in the fact that, given where we are, etc., having just got off the plane, and other things being equal and circumstances normal, we do as a matter of course, of custom, of convention, turn right on seeing the sign. And our doing it as a matter of course, or custom, or convention, means that we are, for example, prepared to correct ourselves and others when we inadvertently turn the wrong way, and that we react differently to the inadvertence of others than we do to their ignorance. And, again, that, unless we are, for example joking or meaning to deceive, we give certain sorts of answers to questions as to why we are moving as we are; we say, 'Because that's the way to go; didn't you see the sign?' And that we question the irregular behaviour of others in certain ways: 'Didn't she see . . .? Didn't she realize . . .? Didn't she *want* to get out of the building . . . ?' In short, and in general, our understanding consists in the fact that we are totally at home with that complex, articulated mode of activity in which the sign plays its role. We have this activity under the belt, its manœuvres and their various interrelations are natural to us, we have mastered this game.

But, it might still be objected, *this* surely cannot be the bedrock of our understanding—for all this needs explaining. *How* is it that we know our way around in this activity, that we are prepared to correct mistakes in certain ways and to ask and answer questions predictably, etc.? Isn't it *because we understand* what the sign means, and isn't that understanding of ours therefore something that lies hidden behind this complicated surface activity?

There is an illusion here. Certainly our mastery of the activity needs to be accounted for. And, further, the account we give must display the turning-right behaviour to be rule-following, and not, for example mechanical or instinctive, or coerced, or due to inclination. But that does not mean that therefore the account will be *in terms of* our understanding the sign, as opposed to being in terms of mechanical features, or whatever. On the contrary; what we need is an account *of* our mastery, of our being in a position to do what we do when we see the sign, of our being able to correct others, and so on. This will be precisely an account *of* our understanding the sign. Understanding will be the *explanandum*, not the *explanans*.

What, then, is the account of our understanding, of our mastery, of our being able, unlike the foreign visitor, to do what we do on seeing the sign, of our being able to correct others, etc.? Well, we, unlike the visitor, were brought up with signs of this kind. We were initiated into the practice—not, of course, by being instructed as to the meaning of the sign, by having it interpreted for us (e.g. 'that (pointing) means "turn right" '). This again is where we were before; no such instruction can produce under-standing *ab initio*, since it presupposes understanding. We were initiated into the practice by what Wittgenstein (and indeed Kant)[10] calls *training (abrichten)*. We were, for example, repeatedly led by the hand as our elders followed the sign; we mimicked or made random moves, and were guided and corrected, encouraged and re-strained, with nods and gestures at the sign, and talk of various kinds: 'No, not that way; look, the arrow is telling us which way to go, let's go that way' (and they go, hand-in-hand), etc., etc. Of course, all this can be as varied as you please, and it all takes time. And of course, some of us may have learned the sign by instruction after all ('the arrow means go to the right', or '→' means ' ⊃ ')—*if*, that is, we already had the practice but were un-familiar with the particular sign. In which case the instrument of training would have been not the arrow, but the horseshoe, or the words, or whatever it was that had initially served in our practice.

It is, then, our upbringing, our training, that accounts for our mastery of the practice, for our behaving as we do with respect to the sign. It is this that explains our rule-following actions. One's understanding (e.g. of what to do on seeing the sign) is constituted, we have argued, by one's mastery of the practice. Below, independently of, the practice there is no understanding, and so there can be no account of one's mastery of the practice in terms of what one understands—no explanation of one's rule-following behaviour (e.g. turning right) in terms of one's awareness of something (of what one recognizes the sign to mean). An account 'from below' is pernicious when it appeals to something that lies beneath the bedrock of understanding or awareness as something of which one is nevertheless aware, that is something *for one*. This, we saw, was Kant's problem in locating the categories. Such accounts attempt to explain one's rule-following actions in terms of one's awareness of the rules, where that awareness is something quite distinct from the actions that express it. This sort of account, we

[10] See A134/B173a.

have argued (both with respect to Kant and generally)
cannot succeed. But the present account, from training,
is not of this kind. It does not attempt to ground one's
rule-following actions in what one understands; rather, it
sees one's capacity to perform those actions (one's
mastery of the practice) as *constituting* one's awareness
of the rules, and provides a natural account (not grounds)
of how one might have come to have such mastery.[11] It is
not as if my grounds for behaving as I do is my belief that
I was brought up in a certain way. What is true is merely
that in general, and so doubtless in my case too, such
mastery is brought about, if at all, by such upbringing.

But what is this mastery that such an upbringing
brings about? Isn't it just a tendency or proclivity to
behave in certain ways? And how can that involve
consciousness of rules, or of anything? How can it
contain a for-me factor? Isn't it another form of behaviourism once again? In order to try to answer these
questions we need to piece together the main points of
our present inquiry.

A central purpose of the present chapter has been to
make intelligible the idea of a consciousness of rules that
is *essentially implicit*. This is the idea of an awareness of
rules which is involved in a given action or enterprise,
but which cannot be separated from that action or
enterprise and cannot therefore be seen as presupposed
by it or underlying it. The idea of this implicit rule-
consciousness is not simply a curiosity which it would
be intellectually satisfying to have explained. It is, we
have argued, crucial both to Kant's main argument in the
Transcendental Deduction, and to the intelligibility of
rule-following behaviour in general.

We saw earlier that the categories, if they are to
function as Kant would have them function, must be *in*
our consciousness (and not below its threshold, where we
are blind) without however being objects of that consciousness, items *of* which we are aware (for they are the
rules, the acting on which makes consciousness of

---

[11] This natural account answers what Kant calls the *quid facti* question,
that of how we in fact come to exercise this capacity (A84/B116 ff.).

anything possible). So we need to find room for the idea of an awareness of rules which is somehow implicit in our awareness of anything. But Kant's picture of the conscious mind contains no such room; it, like Descartes's, lacks the dimension necessary for anything in consciousness that is not an object of consciousness, for anything in thinking that is not being thought. This revealed to us the need for a broader conception of consciousness (which, we noted but did not pursue, already contained the idea of communicability), the conception of an act of thinking that included, but did not reduce to, a first-person point of view. Such an act of thinking, we suggested, could be nothing other than an act of speech.

Now, so far as the argument to that point goes, this idea of an essentially implicit rule-consciousness, and its implications, seems to be nothing more than a requirement of Kant's theory. Nothing, so far, argues for its plausibility except the plausibility of Kant's own argument: if intentional consciousness contains a for-me factor, and if that factor cannot be accounted for except by means of a spontaneous act, etc., then . . . But this, as we saw, is not the end of the story, for if we pursue the idea of rule-following on its own account, quite independently of Kantian theory, we find precisely the same situation, the same need for a rule-consciousness that is essentially implicit in something else. Explicit rule-consciousness, where the rules are the objects of thought, can be no more fundamental in real life than it can be in Kant, and it cannot play a role in explicating what it is to act on a rule. If we are to understand rule-following at all we must see the awareness of rules that it contains not as a phenomenon in its own right, an isolatable element in consciousness, but as essentially embodied in something larger. But now, in considering rule-following generally, outside the narrow confines of Kant's theory, we can see much more clearly and much more fully than we could with Kant *what that larger something is* in which the consciousness of rules is embodied. With Kant the embodying act is 'judging', always and only judging. In actual cases of rule-following we have multi-dimensional, less purely intellectual examples: moving the bishop in chess, going by a signpost, obeying an order, as well as judging something to be red, or a cube, or that 1002 comes after 1000 in the plus-2 series. While we confine ourselves to judging, and especially to judging-in-general, it is extremely difficult to arrive at a clear sense that what we have here is an *embodying* act at all—something that can be seen as implicitly containing within it, but not as a separable ingredient, one's consciousness of the rules. Judging has no evident *body* at all; to judge, it seems, is to do nothing more than to think that *p*, to be aware that *p*. And how, one might ask, can one's awareness that *p*, regarded merely as such, contain one's awareness of rules (or of anything) except as an ingredient, that is *explicitly*? It is here that the dimension is lacking, in Kant, for that final break with the Cartesian picture of consciousness that his theory demands.

Attending to acts like going by a signpost, or moving the bishop in chess, makes it possible to see how the demands of the theory can be met. Attending to the act of judging-in-general does not do this. What is the crucial difference here? Well, one might start by pointing out that whereas to judge *is* to be aware that so-and-so (and therefore judging cannot implicitly contain the awareness of anything) going by the signpost is clearly not *itself* being aware of anything (and so can, in principle, contain such awareness implicitly). This, though true enough as far as it goes, is certainly not sufficient and indeed points in a dangerous direction. For it suggests that whereas judging is itself an act of consciousness (and so could not include another such act except as an ingredient, and thus explicitly)—going by the sign is not itself an act of consciousness, but a physical movement, a piece of bodily behaviour, and so could contain what is needed, the implicit awareness of rules. But now we have the question of what 'contain' could possibly mean here, of what the relation between the physical movement and the awareness of the rule could possibly be. It is not, surely, as if the awareness of the rule is an actual part of the physical act of turning right. Is it then that the physical act is accompanied by the awareness of the rule? Or is it that the awareness of the rule is an element in a larger, psychophysical act of turning-right-in-certain-circumstances? Without going into this further (this is a Pandora's box for the philosophy of mind!) I think it is clear that whatever could enter into any such relations with the physical act of turning right it would not be an essentially implicit awareness of the rule. Whatever accompanied the act, or formed a part of it, would have to be actually there, explicitly present. And it is absolutely crucial that one's awareness of the rules be essentially implicit in what one does, if one's actions are to be coherently seen as rule-following. This has been our argument in the latter part of the present chapter. Nothing that is present to consciousness can, by being added to or combined with a piece of behaviour, make that piece of behaviour rule-following.

So, if the only way in which rule-consciousness can relate to a physical act (e.g. of turning right on seeing the sign) is by being conjoined with it, and so by being explicit, and if rule-consciousness must basically be an implicit affair, then it follows that the physical act itself, the piece of bodily behaviour, is not a sufficient embodiment of rule-consciousness. An act, a movement, anything that happens in a time-slice, cannot, taken in isolation, constitute rule-following behaviour, precisely because it contains no room for implicit awareness of rules. We cannot find rule-consciousness in a time-slice at all. The attempt to find it there leads only to unresolvable disputes between dualism on the one hand and one or another brand of monism. For if rule-consciousness exists, in its basic, paradigmatic form, here and now (pointing at the person moving the bishop), then it must either *be* the movement indicated (behaviourism), or one or another item that exists alongside that movement (e.g. an inner state, or a state of the brain).

But to say that rule-consciousness cannot be found in a time-slice is not to deny that one can at a given time, here and now, be conscious of the rule; for there *is* such a thing, derivatively, as explicit rule-consciousness. Nor is it to deny that rule-consciousness is expressed precisely by such acts as moving the bishop along the diagonal, or turning right. What is being denied is that we can find *in the time-slice* what it is that makes such acts the rule-following actions that they are.

So we must look beyond the time-slice in which the act (moving the bishop, turning right) occurs to see the awareness of the rule—and yet we must see the act itself as (typically, but not necessarily, since one can perform the act without knowing the rule) expressing that awareness. But to look beyond the time-slice in which the act occurs, while still focusing in this way on the act itself would be presumably to look at the context, the circumstances, in which the act occurs. (It is, after all, only in certain circumstances, as we saw, that turning right on seeing the sign displays an awareness of the rule.) But now we must take care not to make the same mistake again, and regard the circumstances as a larger compound, in which both physical act and awareness of the rule are atomic elements. For then again there will be no way of seeing rule-consciousness as anything but explicit. This means that by 'circumstances' we do not mean 'spatio-temporal circumstances' (the larger compound), as if we should broaden our search beyond the act, but, as it were, in the same dimensions; as if we should indiscriminately include everything in space surrounding the person performing the act (up to how many feet?) and everything that preceded and succeeded it (up to how many minutes, or hours?).

We know that rule-consciousness cannot be a phenomenon in its own right underlying rule-following behaviour, but must be fundamentally a practical affair, essentially implicit in, having its very being in, behaviour. We now know also that such consciousness cannot be identified with anything occurrent, either with any piece of behaviour as such or with any element in a pattern of behaviour. We must look beyond actual occurrences. This seems to leave us with only one possibility—that of

identifying the awareness of rules with the entire pattern
of behaviour at issue. This would be accomplished by
attributing the pattern to the agent. To be aware of the
rules would then be, somehow, to *possess* that pattern of
behaviour. Such possession would not of course be a
matter of the agent's being conscious of the pattern, nor
of his being in a certain physiological state,[12] but would
consist simply in its being true—no doubt as a result of
training—that the agent *will* exhibit the pattern, in all its
complexity, *if* placed in appropriate circumstances. For
example, he will turn right on seeing the sign, unless the
circumstances are *w*, in which case he will . . ., and so on.
In this way, so it might be argued, a pattern of behaviour
can embody implicit rule-consciousness by its being the
case that to be conscious of the rules is precisely to have
the complex disposition to exhibit the pattern. To have
mastered the practice is nothing more nor less than to
have acquired the disposition.

As an answer to our question about the nature of rule-
consciousness, this dispositional view seems to have
clear advantages over the other views we have considered. Notably, it seems to make room for the idea that
awareness of rules is not a phenomenon in its own
independent right, standing in some productive or otherwise explanatory relation to behaviour, but is essentially
implicit in, expressed by, how we behave.

But there seems to be something missing in this
dispositional account of the nature of rule-consciousness. It still has the air, associated with all this talk about
behaviour, of being a *reduction* of consciousness to
behaviour. For where in this account, we will want to
ask, are we to find the element of consciousness itself—
what in the account reveals that the rules are something
for the agent—where is the first-person perspective?
Another way of phrasing this question is to ask where, in
this dispositional story, is there room for *explicit* rule-
consciousness. For while it is indeed essential to the

---

[12] For then rule-consciousness would not be a basically practical matter,
and so there would again be the question of *connecting* the conscious, or
physiological, state *to* the behaviour.

business of rule-following that the awareness of rules be fundamentally implicit in one's behaviour, it seems to be equally necessary that the one who is following the rule be *capable* of bringing the rule to consciousness—that is, of representing the rule to himself, of having a thought of the form 'I'm supposed to turn right'. If this capability is not built into the agent's possessing the pattern of behaviour, then his possessing it does not seem to qualify as his being aware of anything at all.

But perhaps the dispositional account of rule-consciousness can accommodate this requirement of a first-person perspective. The disposition at issue is, it will be said, not simple, but richly complex. Someone who has acquired it will not only (*ceteris paribus*) turn right on seeing the sign (as if mechanically induced to do so), but will also (*ceteris paribus*) say certain things when asked certain questions. In particular, if asked why he behaved as he did, why he turned right at that point, he will say something to the effect that he saw a sign pointing that way, telling him to go that way—thereby making explicit his awareness of the rule. His talk *shows* that the sign's telling him to turn right is a situation for him, it manifests his awareness of the rule in first-person terms.

I do not think that this sort of manœuvre dispels the uneasiness one feels about the dispositional account of rule-consciousness. It is not that one would want to dispute the last claim made, that these sorts of answers on the agent's part show his awareness of the rule. It is rather that as a product of the dispositional account this claim has the air of a *deus ex machina*, and is unconvincing. It is as if it were being conceded that everything else in the account—all the other things the agent is disposed to do—is compatible with his being a wound-up mechanism (where training is the key),[13] whereas as soon as he makes certain verbal utterances something quite different, namely understanding, is revealed. But if the uttering of these vocables is just something else that the agent, as a result of training, is disposed to do, where his

---

[13] And why *not* identify the actual having of the disposition with a physiological state, perhaps one that is yet to be discovered?

being so disposed is exactly on a level with all the other things he is disposed to do, as the account must insist that it is, why should there be this remarkable and radical difference? As far as the dispositional account goes, verbal behaviour is just as much *just behaviour* as any other. If, on the other hand, one wants to say that there isn't really this radical difference: the non-verbal behaviour, as much as the verbal, demonstrates the agent's awareness of the rule, then the correct response, it seems to me, is that the dispositional account altogether fails to bring this out. It is not convincing to be told that the mere fact that if placed in circumstances *c* one will, other things being equal, do *a*, *essentially* brings in consciousness. To persuade us that it is talking about consciousness of the rule, the dispositional account aligns non-verbal behaviour to verbal behaviour; to assure us that such consciousness is not a separate phenomenon but has its whole being *in* behaviour, the account aligns verbal behaviour to non-verbal behaviour. It cannot do both at once.

But now it might well look as if we have exhausted all possibilities as far as the nature of rule-consciousness, and therefore of rule-following, goes. We have seen that awareness of a rule, though indeed a situation for one and so not identifiable as anything lying below the level of consciousness, cannot be identified as an item in consciousness, underlying behaviour. We have seen further that such awareness cannot be identified with any piece of behaviour, and indeed with any occurring phenomenon. We were thus led to thinking that such awareness might be the dispositional possession of a whole pattern of behaviour. This account too has foundered. And it has foundered, like the earlier accounts, on the dual requirement that rule-consciousness *both* be a situation for one and at the same time that it have its whole being in how one behaves. It seems impossible to satisfy both of these requirements at once. How can something that is essentially *practical* be a situation *for one*? How, conversely, can the first-person perspective have its home in *behaviour*?

I think there is a way out of this impasse. We have argued that rule-consciousness is not itself a discrete phenomenon but must be contained in something larger. We have called this larger phenomenon a practice, and we have encouraged the view that rule-consciousness, that irreducibly practical knowledge that we are trying to identify, is nothing but the mastery of such a practice. This talk, of practice and of mastery, does not itself of course solve our problem. For we still have the question as to what a practice is and what mastery of a practice amounts to. Is a practice, for example, a concatenation of human actions, a pattern of behaviour, and is mastery of a practice a disposition to exhibit such a pattern? We have found the dispositionalist account unconvincing. But just where does the dispositionalist go wrong? He is right, after all, in claiming that to regard someone as aware of a rule, as, for example, knowing what to do on seeing the sign →, is, *somehow*, to attribute a complex pattern of actions to him. And, further, the dispositionalist is right in thinking that to regard someone as knowing what to do is to attribute that pattern to him, in advance of his performing the actions in question. (It is not as if the agent knows what to do only when actually doing it). The dispositionalist is also right in seeing the need to avoid the manœuvre of attributing the actions (that compose the pattern) to the agent via the attribution of a representation, an idea, of those actions to him. (Knowing what to do on seeing the sign does not consist in the occurrence of any formula in the agent's mind). The attribution of the action(s) to the agent cannot be mediated, it must be direct. But—and this is what the dispositionalist does not see—the fact that the actions must, somehow, be attributed to the agent directly, without mediation, does not prevent their being *inflected* in a certain way. For this is precisely what we need; we need to see the actions attributed to the agent not as actions *simpliciter*, whatever that might mean, nor as things that people do or might do, or that they would do if . . . , but as things TO DO. My claim, then, is this; that a practice is indeed a network of actions, but it is not one of actions in assertoric or hypothetical form, or of actions 'as such', but of actions in *gerundive* form, of things to do. It is *only* if we see a practice in this way, that is, if we see behaviour, the practical, in this way, that we can make sense of the idea that rule-consciousness is irreducibly practical, essentially implicit in our behaviour.

Consider a specific practice, the game of chess. What we are claiming with respect to its ontological status is this. Chess is not (a) a network of movements neutrally or factually described (the bishop along the diagonal, the rook parallel to the sides of the board). Nor is it (b) a network of such movements, so described, to which the conformity to rules has been added (this would be the external rule-governedness we talked of earlier in this chapter). Nor again is chess (c) a network of movements, neutrally described, each of which is underlain by, and made as a result of, an awareness that one is to make that movement in that way. The game of chess is a complex, not of *movements made*, actually or potentially, accompanied or unaccompanied by consciousness, but of *moves to be made*. And these moves-to-be-made are themselves basic items. They are not metaphysical constructs, out of physical movements on the one hand and rules on the other. And mastery of the game, correlatively, is not a matter of one's actually making those movements, or of one's potentially doing so, that is of one's being triggerable, by the stimulus of circumstances, to make them (dispositionalism); it is a matter of one's having the moves (what to do when) under one's belt.

To say that a practice, a rule-governed enterprise, like the game of chess, is made up of things to do, of gerundive actions, is itself uncontroversial. For something to be (internally) rule-governed *is* for it to be a move to be made or to consist of moves to be made. The interesting question is not whether a practice is a complex of gerundive actions but whether it is so in the final analysis, whether this characterization of a practice is the fundamental one. Our Cartesian tendencies urge us to break things down further: a thing to do is a doing, subject to a rule—so we have two distinct items, a doing (e.g. a physical movement) and a rule. And to follow a rule, to do the thing to do, is to make the movement in the light of the rule; so again we have two items, the movement and the consciousness of the rule. It is Wittgenstein's achievement to have shown the futility of this attempt at analysis. The lesson of this chapter which owes its nerve to Wittgenstein, is that we must resist this atomization of rule-following behaviour. But to resist the atomization is not first to accept it and then to reduce the resultant duality to a unity, by excluding one of its two constituents (consciousness) and focusing only on the other (behaviour). This was the strategy of dispositionalism. To resist the atomization is to regard rule-following behaviour as *fundamentally* what it first presents itself as being, a matter of doing the thing to do.

Conclusion

We began the previous chapter with the recognition that
Kant's argument in the Transcendental Deduction was
unable to show what it was designed to show, namely
that only those acts of judgment which are expressed in
the public language—acts of judgment by means of the
categories—could succeed in uniting data in such a way
as to produce consciousness of objects. All that Kant
could show, it seemed, was that whatever kind of act it is
that affords intentional consciousness, it must meet the
same formal conditions that are required for those
publicly communicable acts, it must be spontaneous and
rule-governed. But to allow this, and even to allow, as we
did, that our only model for acts of the required kind are
the acts performed in the public language, is not
sufficient to establish the claim in question. We need, in
particular, an explanation as to why it is that one's
ability to perform communicable acts should be thought
to be a necessary condition of one's (solitary) consciousness of anything. Why should there not be acts productive of intentional consciousness which are both rule-
governed and 'private', intelligible only to the person
whose acts they are? Why should, and how can, those
conditions which happen to be necessary for mutually
intelligible speech be necessary for consciousness itself? I
believe our discussion of the nature of rule-following in
Chapter 6 provides us with answers to these questions.
  While we continue to see understanding or intentional
consciousness as having at its unexplained and unanalys-
able basis *one's representing things to oneself as thus
and so*, then it will seem impossible that consciousness
should *by its very nature* be communicable. On the

contrary, the communicability of understanding will seem to be something extra, something that is itself deeply problematic, and standing in need of an explanation as to how it is possible. The demon of privacy has its home, and I think its only home, in this Cartesian picture, in the idea that representing something to oneself is something quite fundamental which lies on the bedrock of understanding.

A major consequence of our argument in Chapter 6 is that rule-consciousness, the acceptance of rules as governing one's behaviour, is not, at bottom, a *representational* matter at all. To act on one's understanding of the rule is not for one's action to be underlain by, or accompanied by, an *idea* of what one is to do; rather, it is for one's action to proceed directly, without representational mediation, from one's mastery of the practice. Now it seems to me that there is no place in this scenario for the demon of privacy to gain a foothold. For to suppose that the rule being followed might be private, intelligible only to the person following it, is to suppose that that person's awareness of the rule is a discrete phenomenon in its own right, something whose fundamental character is a presence to the mind. Only if the rule is looked upon this way, as something the understanding of which consists in what is to be done *being represented to me*, does it make sense to wonder whether *my* understanding of what is to be done might not after all, be private to me, despite the overall conformity of my behaviour to that of others. This threat of privacy exists only if rule-consciousness is taken to be fundamentally explicit, only if understanding what one is to do is basically a matter of giving oneself an interpretation of what one is to do. But if, as we have argued, rule-consciousness, understanding what one is to do, is irreducibly practical, consisting in one's having practical mastery of the network of gerunds, then there is no room for the supposition that my understanding might be unique, even though my behaviour conforms with that of others.

So the question as to why the conditions for com-

municating one's understanding or consciousness of
something should also be the conditions of one's being
(solitarily) conscious of it is answered in the following
way. There is no such thing as understanding or being
conscious of something where such understanding or
consciousness is divorced from the conditions of its
communicability. Understanding the directional sign,
knowing what to do on seeing it, is to have mastered a
practice, to have under one's belt a complex network of
moves to be made. And those moves are precisely those
which, when someone makes them, show, make public,
communicate the fact, that he understands the sign:
moves like turning right, correcting others ('No, not that
way'); explaining one's behaviour ('The sign pointed this
way'), and so on, and so forth. They would not be relevant
moves if they did not show this. To understand the sign
is to have mastered the language-game we communally
play with it.

Suppose, now, that we are more-or-less satisfied with
this account of understanding in this sort of case.
Understanding such things as a pointing sign is at bottom
a wholly practical matter, there is no basic representational component. (Though there is, and essentially, a
derivative representational component. It is necessary
that explicit rule-consciousness is possible (B131).) Now,
granting all this, it might look as if there is still a
question of aligning this result with Kant. And it might
be thought that we are debarred from applying what we
have learned here to Kant's problem precisely because
Kant is concerned with a quite different kind of understanding. He is concerned, it will be said, with *Erkenntnis*,
theoretical knowledge, with our understanding *things to
be thus and so*—not with our understanding *what we are
to do*. The fact, granting that it is one, that the latter is
irreducibly practical hardly proves that the former is so
also.

There is, of course, something right about this, but as
an objection it does not do justice to the issues. For Kant
insists that all acts of the understanding are spontaneous
and rule-governed, and we have argued in general that an

action can be rule-governed only if it is made as a move in a practice which one has mastered. What needs to be recognized is that one's understanding that such and such is the case (e.g. that this is red, that that is a dog) is *as fully a fundamentally practical matter* as is one's understanding that this or that is what one is to do (e.g. turn right). The connection between understanding and behaviour is equally strong in both cases. Just as my understanding the arrow to be a directional sign is expressed in my turning right, correcting others, etc., so my understanding this to be red is expressed by my picking it up, when I have been looking for something red, by my pointing to it or fetching it, when asked to indicate or produce something red, by my correcting others, and so on. And if we regard understanding-this-to-be-red as fundamentally a representational matter, as being a mental *Urphänomen*, then we run into precisely the same difficulties that confronted us when we regarded understanding-the-pointing-sign in this way. There will once again be an unbridgeable gap between the understanding and any action that is to express it, for once again the mental phenomenon alleged to constitute understanding will itself need to be understood. The moral here is this: unless we are prepared to give up altogether the idea *that understanding can be expressed in behaviour*, we cannot identify understanding with any mental phenomenon. And this is as true when the understanding is 'propositional' as when it is overtly practical. If understanding can be expressed in action at all, there is no understanding which is at bottom a representational event, an explicit grasping in consciousness.

The difference between understanding that this is red and understanding the directional sign is not, then, a difference between the theoretical (or representational) and the practical; it is no more than the difference between different practices. To see something as red is to have mastered a different (though partially overlapping) set of gerunds than the set one has mastered in seeing something to be a signpost.

At the root of Kant's failure to solve the problem of the Transcendental Deduction is the fact that, though he has committed himself to rejecting the Cartesian picture of consciousness, he does not succeed in completely doing so. That he is committed to rejecting it is evident from his insistence that the possibility of representing any-thing as a situation for one (the analytic unity of consciousness) needs to be accounted for. The 'I think', the fact of representing something to oneself, the first-person perspective, is not a given, not something funda-mental in the understanding, but needs to be explained in terms of something else, something 'deeper' in the understanding. He argues that the 'I think' is underlain by a spontaneous act of synthesis. The trouble is that he provides us with no way of seeing what this act is other than an act of pure thinking ('judging'). But such an act is simply an act *of* representing things to oneself as being thus and so, that is, an act that is itself performed *from* a first-person perspective. So Kant's attempt to ground the 'I think' in something deeper in the understanding could not succeed.

We are now in a position to see that such acts of pure thinking, for example of saying 'Turn right', or 'That's red' to oneself, are nothing other than instances of what we have called explicit rule-consciousness. This means, given our argument, that they are not fundamental self-explanatory acts of pure understanding, but moves that are themselves to be explained *in terms of one's under-standing*, in terms, that is, of one's mastery of the practice.

Our subject in this book has been Kant's theory of human understanding, his account of the nature of our awareness of the world. And we have been concerned, in particular, with three important theses or convictions, on Kant's part, that propel that account and which we set out in the introduction to this book. I paraphrase them here.

1. Human understanding is essentially something underived; neither our consciousness of things nor our

capacity to form concepts of them can be explained by reference to any confrontation that we might have with them. In particular, there is no consciousness of anything that consists simply in our being sensorily affected, and there is no concept so basic, no idea so 'simple', that it arises merely from our receiving sense-impressions. The understanding is from first to last 'spontaneous'.

2. Despite its spontaneity, our understanding is not cut loose from its objects. It is, by its own nature, capable of attaching to just those things we see and touch which themselves cannot, according to 1, be regarded as responsible for it.

3. Our understanding is essentially expressible in the language with which we communicate with one another. There is no understanding which does not obey the rules or conditions governing the mutual intelligibility of what we say. It is not something extraneous to the fact of our understanding that we are able to express that understanding by following those rules.

In this book we have tried to make out two things. First, we have tried to show that Kant's picture of the understanding is inadequate to the demands that these three theses place upon it. Secondly, we have indicated how understanding must be conceived if those demands are to be met.

Kant, we have persistently argued, is unable to articulate the connections between the various aspects or dimensions of understanding, unable to show, that is, how the different elements (the horizontal and vertical aspects, rule-governedness and communicability) all belong together in the unitary capacity that is called understanding. We have in his theory what amounts to three separate accounts, the products of which are declared, but not shown, by Kant to be inseparable. First, the account of the conditions or rules for mutually intelligible sentence formation; secondly, the account of the conditions of application; and thirdly, the account of the conditions of anything's being present to consciousness. But it is not enough to declare the products of these three accounts to be one thing, unless one can provide a way of seeing that they can be so. And this Kant cannot do. For all his protests, the three capacities he has isolated remain in principle distinct and separate: the capacity to put words together to form sentences of the public language (the Clue), the capacity to think in spatio-temporal terms (the Schematism), and the capacity to bring explicitly to consciousness (the Deduction).

Nor, we should add, is it enough to say that these three capacities, distinct in themselves, must exist together in anyone who *understands*—that we won't count someone as understanding unless he can do all three of these things. This again will not be enough, for unless we can show what it is about these three capacities that requires that they belong together, the claim that they do will seem arbitrary and conventional ('we count someone as understanding only if . . .'). And this leaves the door open for rejecting the convention and claiming that really, basically, understanding already exists in the exercise of the third of those capacities alone: human understanding is at bottom a matter of presence to consciousness. And so we are left with the Cartesian picture.

The positive argument of this book has been that the conditions that Kant lays down for understanding can be met if, and only if, understanding is conceived as fundamentally a practical affair. To understand *is* to have mastered a network of things to do. The three capacities at issue are to be seen as abstractions from that unitary mastery. They exist and are connected with one another in, and only in, the practice.

INDEX

Analytic of Concepts 6, 9, 10
Analytic of Principles 6, 9, 10
analytic unity of apperception,
    of consciousness 89, 91–
    4, 98 n., 166
apperception
    faculty of 3 n., 91
    and consciousness of objects
        66, 69–71, 89, 92–3, 102,
        107–9, 112, 124, 131,
        134–5, 137–8
Aristotle 22
autonomy (of understanding)
    1, 102, 124–6
awareness of objects, *see*
    consciousness of objects

behaviourism 144, 151
Bennett, Jonathan 6–12, 14,
    33
Berkeley, G. 55
'blindness' 24, 35, 55–7, 66–7,
    121, 123–4, 126–7, 142

Cartesian picture of conscious-
    ness 4, 5, 130, 132–4,
    160–1, 163, 166, 168
categories
    and schemata 8–9, 26–30,
        59, 111–12, 127
    and judgment forms 14–
        20, 26–8, 54
    and consciousness of objects
        54–7, 61–2, 69, 73, 82, 87,
        107, 109, 113, 115–17,
        128, 134

and language 56, 96, 110, 115
    as lying below apperception
        126–8, 137, 151
chess 136–7, 139, 153, 160
Chipman, L. 7 n., 38
chromatic affection 77, 79–
    80, 94–6
Clue (to the Discovery of all
    Pure Concepts of the
    Understanding) 4, 5, 12,
    49, 51–8, 87–8, 96, 100,
    102, 109, 110, 168
    see also metaphysical
        deduction
coherence, of a thought, *see*
    unity of a thought
combination, *see*
    synthesis
'common root' (of sensibility
    and understanding) 31, 48
communicability, of thought,
    of consciousness 99, 104–
    5, 111, 119, 132, 134,
    162–3, 167
concepts
    and consciousness of objects
        2, 91–4
    and categories 8–11, 16–21,
        28, 76
conceptus communis 91, 92
consciousness of objects,
    intentional consciousness
        1–4, 34–5, 43, 61, 71–112
        passim, 113–68 *passim*
    see also apperception, for-
        me factor

Critique of Judgment 76

Deduction, *see* Transcendental Deduction
denken 57 n.
Descartes, R. 2, 4, 23, 25, 71, 75, 83, 89, 129, 152
'determine' (an object) 18–19, 21–2, 25, 28, 30, 32, 40, 51, 59
dispositionalism 156–61
duality, of concept-possession 9–11, 22–3, 29–32, 36–8, 42

ego-reflexive perspective 129–30
empiricism, empiricist(s) 1, 55–6, 69–70, 87, 109, 113–16
Erfahrung 57 n.
erkennen 4 n., 57 n.
Erkenntnis 4 n., 57 n., 107, 164
explicit (rule-consciousness) 137, 139–41, 143, 144–5, 152–6

faculty-psychology 3 n., 127
First Analogy 18 n.
first-person (perspective, point of view) 72–5, 79–80, 129–33, 148, 157, 158
for-me factor 70, 74, 77, 80–90, 93, 97, 98, 101–6, 114, 116, 117, 118, 120–9, 131–5, 138
forms of judgment 13–22, 26, 28, 51–4
    see also functions of unity, logical forms
'from below' (of explanations) 112, 127–8, 137, 147

functions of thought, of understanding, of unity 8, 14, 15, 17, 19, 21, 22, 24–6, 29–30, 33–5, 42, 47, 51, 53, 57, 59, 87–8, 95–6

general logic 15
gerund, gerundive form 160, 163, 165
grammar, grammatical (in Wittgenstein) 45–6
Guyer, P. 63–9, 74, 78–9

Herz, M. 66 n.
horizontal (capacity) 15, 19, 24–5, 29, 34–41, 167
    see also vertical
Hume, D. 2, 23, 24, 55, 62, 70, 87, 89, 109

'I think' 62–3, 78, 81, 82–6, 89, 92, 93, 98, 106, 115, 130, 166
idealist 1
implicit (rule-consciousness) 137–41, 145, 151–6
intentional consciousness, *see* consciousness of objects
intentional object, object of consciousness 17, 35, 57 n., 68–9, 72–80, 83–90, 119, 129, 133, 138, 152
interpretation (of a rule) 145, 147, 163
intuition 9, 17, 23–4, 34–5, 43–4, 46, 50–1, 53, 56, 58, 66, 67, 93 n., 104, 107

judgment
    faculty of 6, 8, 9, 11, 53

as act of understanding 53,
56–7, 82, 86–7, 107–10,
131, 134, 152–3, 162, 166
forms of, *see* forms of
judgment

Kemp Smith, N. 57 n., 62 n.
Kripke, S. 144

language, in relation to
consciousness 2, 97, 99,
102–4, 110–12, 114–15
language-game 40–7
Leibniz, G. W. 2, 127
Locke, J. 2, 22 n., 70, 87, 100,
127, 133
logical forms, logical
functions 8, 14, 17, 26,
28, 29, 32, 33, 52–7,
107–9
see also forms of judgment,
functions of unity

manifold, of intuition 17, 51,
99, 107, 109
mastery, of language-game,
practice, technique 41,
47–8, 135, 149, 150–1,
160, 163–6, 168
Meiklejohn, J. 57 n.
metaphysical deduction 5, 12,
28
see also Clue
Müller, F. M. 57 n.

object of consciousness, of
thought, *see* intentional
object
objective validity, of the
categories 50–1, 57–60

paradox, of rule-
governedness, etc. 124–6,
128, 135

perceptio 75
Phenomena and Noumena
8 n.
Plato 23
practical knowledge 135, 155,
158–60, 163–5
practice, *see* mastery
Prichard, H. A. 6 n.
Principles (of Pure
Understanding) 12 n., 96
privacy
of understanding 99, 101–
5, 116–21, 131, 162–3
of language 100
Prolegomena 8 n., 85 n.
public language 97, 99, 100,
102–3, 105, 112, 116–17,
119, 127, 131, 134, 162

'quid facti' 151 n.
'quid juris' 58

REMs 64–5
rationalist(s) 1
realist(s) 1
repraesentatio 75
representation
as epitomizing
consciousness 4, 159,
162, 165
v. object of consciousness
65–9, 75, 94, 97
rule-consciousness, rule-
following action 134–61
passim
rule-governedness
of language 55, 100, 102
of understanding 100–7,
114, 116–18, 122–5, 127–
8, 131–2, 134–5, 138, 140,
162, 164–5, 167
Russell, B. 42 n.
Ryle, G. 76

schemata 9, 20, 26–30, 59,
111–12, 127
Schematism 4–7, 9–10, 17,
20, 22, 29–30, 48–9, 51,
55, 56, 58, 59, 168
schematized (and
unschematized)
categories 8, 10–12, 18–
22, 26–8, 43, 49, 55, 59,
60
self-ascription 62–9, 78–9
self-consciousness 63–8, 78–
9, 82–3, 106
sensibility 9 n., 31, 50, 62, 66,
68–73, 78, 80, 84–6, 94,
97, 101–3, 113, 115–16,
118, 120, 126–7
sensory affection 2, 61, 69–73,
76–8
sensory state 71, 81
sensus communis 120
sentience 54–5, 61, 71, 75, 80,
82, 86, 98, 99, 113, 123
Sinnlichkeit 57 n.
spontaneous (-eity) 2, 3, 84–6,
90, 100, 102–5, 107, 114,
117, 126, 152, 162, 164,
166, 167
state of consciousness
v. object of consciousness
65, 68, 71–6, 78–9
Strawson, P. F. 6 n., 17 n., 33,
75 n., 106
Stroud, B. 59 n.
subjective conditions of
thought, subjective
necessity 50, 57, 58, 59 n.
synthesis, synthesize 89–91,
95–8, 100–6, 109–10,
114–15, 125, 131, 166

synthetic unity of
apperception, of
consciousness 89, 91, 94

Table of Categories 17, 19, 34
Table of Judgments 13–15, 17,
19
training 42, 150–1, 156
Transcendental Aesthetic 21
Transcendental Analytic 5
transcendental arguments
59 n.
Transcendental Deduction 4,
5, 17 n., 25, 49–52, 54–9,
61–5, 67, 78, 82, 87–9,
96–7, 99–100, 102–3,
106–7, 110, 113, 115, 131,
151, 162, 166, 168

unity
of understanding 3 n.
of a thought 14, 15, 23 n.,
33, 46, 52, 88, 99
of a concept 29, 37, 38
of consciousness 88, 91–4,
97, 102, 107
see also analytic unity,
synthetic unity
Urerkenntnis 54, 61, 113
Urphänomen 4, 143, 146, 165

vertical (capacity) 15, 19, 23–
6, 29, 37–41, 51, 167
vorstellen, Vorstellung 68

Warnock, G. J. 6 n., 37, 40
Wilkerson, T. E. 6 n., 63 n.
Wittgenstein, L. 40, 41, 42 n.,
45–7, 76, 118–19, 122,
131, 135, 140, 144, 145,
148, 150